Setting Healthy Boundaries

Limit What Others Take So You
Have More to Give

*(How to Set Strong and Healthy Boundaries and
Take Control of Your Life)*

Vincent Thomas

Published By **Bella Frost**

Vincent Thomas

All Rights Reserved

Setting Healthy Boundaries: Limit What Others Take So You Have More to Give (How to Set Strong and Healthy Boundaries and Take Control of Your Life)

ISBN 978-1-77485-970-4

No part of this guidebook shall be reproduced in any form without permission in writing from the publisher except in the case of brief quotations embodied in critical articles or reviews.

Legal & Disclaimer

The information contained in this ebook is not designed to replace or take the place of any form of medicine or professional medical advice. The information in this ebook has been provided for educational & entertainment purposes only.

The information contained in this book has been compiled from sources deemed reliable, and it is accurate to the best of the Author's knowledge; however, the Author cannot guarantee its accuracy and validity and cannot be held liable for any errors or omissions. Changes are periodically made to this book. You must consult your doctor or get professional medical advice before using any of the suggested remedies, techniques, or information in this book.

Upon using the information contained in this book, you agree to hold harmless the Author from and against any damages, costs, and expenses, including any legal fees potentially resulting from the application of any of the information provided by this guide. This disclaimer applies to any damages or injury caused by the use and application, whether directly or indirectly, of any advice or information presented, whether for breach of contract, tort, negligence, personal injury, criminal intent, or under any other cause of action.

You agree to accept all risks of using the information presented inside this book. You need to consult a professional medical practitioner in order to ensure you are both able and healthy enough to participate in this program.

Table of contents

chapter 1: Apprehensions While Dating Setting Boundaries 1

Chapter 2: Grooming Yourself In An Abetting Way 13

Chapter 3: Classification Boundaries 24

Chapter 4: Setting Bundaries: Questions Coming Up 37

Chapter 5: Parameters - Setting Healthy Boundaries In Marriage 48

Chapter 6: Personal Boundaries 53

Chapter 7: Emotional Boundaries 58

Chapter 8: Sexual Boundaries Marriage . 62

Chapter 9: Boundaries In Marriage To Bring A Work/Life Bridge 73

Chapter 10: Digital Boundaries In Marriage 80

Chapter 11: Important Points To Keep In Mind When Setting Boundaries 88

Chapter 12: Boundaries Important For Kids 101

Chapter 13: Boundaries Of Types 106

Chapter 14: Tips To Set Healthy 110

Chapter 15: 7-Step Methodical Process For Setting Healthy Borderies 122

Chapter 16: Difficulties Enthusiasm Setting Boundaries W/Kids 134

Chapter 17: Understanding Bundaries . 143

Chapter 18: On The Lose Without Boundaries 157

Chapter 19: Be Self-Experienced And Build Linearity 171

Chapter 1: Apprehensions While Dating
Setting Boundaries

For some, it might seem contradictory to set boundaries in dating. It's like setting boundaries for the same tiger who you want to run free like a king. It limits your options.

You need to be your best self. If you take a closer look, it isn't so bad. People find it very difficult to fix boundaries during their initial dating phase. It restricts their freedom. They want to have full control over their partners. However, freedom comes at a great cost. If you don't choose to walk this path carefully, you could end up losing important aspects of the rest of your life.

People fear setting boundaries early because they fear it might give the potential date a bad impression. It will. But it will leave an impression that is accurate and it will make your life easier if you ever decide to get married.

People are afraid they might not impress their prospective partners. You may not agree with them, but it is better than falling prey to partners with false expectations and high aspirations.

Here are some things that you should avoid while dating. Also, setting boundaries will be helpful.

Exceeding your limits can cause problems. Be realistic about how much you're willing to show off.

Don't make unrealistic expectations

In order to make their relationship more real, fake or believable, some people are willing to go out of their way. This is a very dangerous but successful and profitable practice. Let us look at this analogy in terms of movies. Although you may enjoy the 30 minute action-packed scene in the trailer, the experience of experiencing that same thrill and nerve-wracking experience throughout the entire movie will be exhausting. You can also imagine how expensive it will be to film the entire movie on the same scale that that trailer. It's a recipe for disaster to set unrealistic expectations and make them impossible to fulfill later. This will cause discontentment in your partner and could lead to ridicule, mockery, and even death.

Dating is not a 100-meter sprint. It is a long relay run. The performance of both partners will directly impact the success or failure the relationship. The collaborative effort is essential. If you begin too quickly and then slow down during the mid, it will get you nowhere. In the beginning, you should establish boundaries and limit how much access you give your date. This is a slow and careful approach but one that will be prudent.

Avoid compromising because of fear of rejection. You must clearly state your needs.

You don't have to be afraid of making a bad impression

For most people, dating is about creating an impression. They are quite correct to a large degree. Dating is about making a lasting impression. It is the reason why courtship is called. If you are the person who is most likely to be a stranger, you need to make sure that they spend at least part of your entire life with you. It is important to show commitment. You need someone who will share your joys, sorrows, and spend time with you. This isn't easy. This is the game where you win over others. This has been happening since before time began. This is the phase that all creatures, human and animal, must go through. To please the potential partner, they have to be happy and there is competition.

Animals seek to impress their partner with their power. Some develop big horns, others have great strength. Even men use power to impress women. Women use beauty, charm and skills to impress men. But, mankind has found many other ways to do it. There are many options available for displaying wealth, status, manners, and etiquettes. Some are just as attractive for their physical appearance, while others can impress their partners with their mental ability.

When people are trying to impress their prospective partners, it is a problem. This applies to both genders. They are constantly misleading themselves and raising expectations. They don't express their desires clearly to the partner. The end result is a incomplete quest. You would soon be looking for other options and the relationship could end. This could be due to your fear about asking the right question, or being judged. This can lead to a poor relationship. Dating isn't about giving up on your dreams. It is the moment when you can be open to your heart without feeling obligated. For the rest of your life, it can be disastrous not to take advantage of this opportunity. It is better for your partner to be clear from this stage. It will save you pain and mental trauma later. Your expectations are also part and parcel of you. They respect your content. A healthy relationship is one where both of the partners respect each others' expectations. They can both be happy. It is not about making someone accept something or bending their will to do so. If you are happy and content with your life, you will be happy.

It will make you feel trapped. This can cause stagnation in a couple. In the dating stage, it is essential to be truthful. You have to say what you want and how it should be done. It is important to express yourself and not be controlled. It's a habit that makes your heart happy and keeps your conscience clear. It can be hard to find the right candidate, as they may not be available. But, not being open about your feelings can lead to discontentment which could cause problems in the future. This applies to both of you. It is important to speak openly and be clear. It is better than to hide the limitations of your expectations and complain later. Also, you must share with your partner the extent of your ability to be accommodating. This will not place any undue pressure on you at a later point.

Don't look desperate. Be realistic about the information you are willing to share.

While important, the company is not everything.

When they first start dating, one of the most common mistakes is to make it seem desperate. They become vulnerable. They are easily exposed to greater levels and can be exploited for weaknesses.

We all have our follies as human beings. You may be in a difficult position if you expose them right away. Your potential partner might see it as an opportunity for you to be exploited. Remember that both you and your potential partner are strangers when you first start dating. It's a way to get to know one another. You can learn to get along with your partner by playing slowly and gently. You get to know each other better and learn to accept the strengths and weaknesses of your potential partner. But if your date knows your stock, then you don't have much to play with. You can also be manipulated. This can make it risky. Haste is not a good quality for establishing a relationship of equality-based partnership.

You should have a clear idea of what you would like your partner to know and what you will tell them later. Plan ahead about the traits and characteristics you want in your partner. It is not wise to make these decisions based on the person you are with. You can be easily deceived by your looks.

It is important to have a partner in your life. But, not all. You need to make compromises in order for your partner to be comfortable with you. However, it is important not give up your rightful control over who your space is. Your dignity and respect for your partner could be at stake if this is not done carefully. They might begin to see you as easygoing and flexible. You may become manipulated and lose control. This is the worst stage of a relationship. However, it is very common. This problem is common in a lot of people. This issue isn't about accepting demands; it is about submissiveness beyond reason.

If a couple doesn't respect their dignity, it won't last. This happens often in relationships that lack healthy boundaries. Slowly but surely, one partner starts manipulating and controlling the space of the other partner. You will lose control over what happens in your life, as well as your partner's. The relationship moves from partnership to master and subordinate, if it is not the slave. Do not be silent about your dislikes or the bad habits in your partner. People find out what they dislike about others. They keep going to put others to the test. You will have to be more accommodating the more you do. Be clear about the things you are willing to do and those you aren't. Do not present yourself as easy to kill. People are more comfortable with the negative things than they are the fear of losing their partner. This fear eventually becomes a shackle. The fear keeps them in a shackle and eventually, the relationship becomes a burden.

It is important for you to define boundaries about the things that you are prepared to accept in your partner, and the things that you don't. It is dangerous to go blind when you are trying to navigate this road of potholes.

Submission can be dangerous. Set limits on how many powers you will share.

Avoid Subletting Your Powers

In a romantic relationship, it is normal to develop a sense of affection. It is natural to want to be with someone you like and to accept their needs. Uncertainty about when to say "No," can be a fatal flaw that could cost you your happiness. There are many important feelings, such as self-esteem and dignity. These feelings should not be subordinated to love. However, you risk letting your future partner have all the power. To love someone else, you have to first love yourself. One shouldn't dehumanize themselves to please another.

Be clear about who can delegate power to you. You must decide what your partner can do on your behalf. Your partner can direct you to follow these things. These are not the things you should follow, but they must be at your partner's request. You should not be blinded by your love for your partner and become a slave to it.

It is important that power exchanges are voluntary and fair. It shouldn't compromise your dignity, self-respect, or your dignity. You should not be afraid of the disapproval from others. There is a fine distinction between being sensitive to the feelings of others and acting as directed. It is important that you recognize it and take steps to avoid getting there.

People will soon realize how easy it is to submit and not resist. Saying no becomes much more difficult.

You can avoid this by being firm in your relationships, especially while you are dating. Limit the power and reach that your partner can have on you so that they don't invade your space. Learn to say no when it is necessary. There shouldn't ever be a temptation to get involved in a new romantic relationship. These situations can be indecisive and will be exploited by those who seek to take advantage.

Chapter 2: Grooming Yourself In An Abetting Way

TO SET BOUNDARIES

To establish boundaries in a dating relationship, you must first prepare yourself. You have to decide what kind relationship you want. Short-term relationships are merely a matter of giving and taking. It's possible to have some excess in your life while still keeping things private. It is important to have clear boundaries when you are looking for relationships. It involves the sharing of information such as personal information, rights, and responsibilities. It is essential to prepare yourself.

Modern life is fast-paced. It doesn't leave much time for thought. Sometimes things don't go according to plan. Relationships often veer off course and sometimes paths diverge. It is vital to define boundaries for important aspects of a relationship such as physical intimacy and commitment.

Before you start a romantic relationship with someone, there are some things you should know.

The Commitment

All relationships are not meant for eternity. Many relationships in the modern age are short-lived. Expecting and pledging the same type of commitment can cause problems. It will become apparent quickly that you are ready to make the commitment in a romantic relationship. This clarity is vital for maturing relationships. It is important to avoid long-term conflict and bad blood later.

Each person has a gut feeling when they enter a relationship. However, this intuition doesn't necessarily turn out to be true every time. This gut feeling is usually driven by physical attraction, and this often fades fast. It is the long-term factors that are most important, such as real feelings, care for one another, hobbies, likes and dislikes, that will matter the most. These are the things you must evaluate quickly. If you want to have a long-term partnership, then you will need to take the time to fully understand your feelings and be able enjoy the process. However, if these feelings are not present to a significant extent, the chances of the relationship lasting long are low. In this case, you need to decide whether or not to reveal certain things.

These days, everyone is connected by social media. Neglecting to set boundaries can result in social shame and disgrace. Both the boyfriend and girlfriend must clearly communicate the seriousness of their relationship and how they intend to move forward.

You should not divulge too many details if you do not intend to take your relationship any further. Both partners need to talk about physical intimacy. It should not be a cause for the partner to drag their relationship along for too long.

There is a lot to be gained from relationships that have a long-term commitment. This is where you need to clearly define your roles and commitments. Be clear on issues like personal space, honesty, and physical intimacy.

The Driving Force

It would be a delusion to think that relationships can only last on a superficial level. The driving force of a relationship in love is often sex. It is thrilling and fresh. It exudes excitement and adventure. The partner is made to feel more comfortable. It is crucial to have physical competence. But the partners need to decide how far they want to go. If a partner doesn't want to have sex with someone else, it is important to communicate this. Understanding if you are only having sex with your partner is crucial. This is crucial as it will impact the duration of the relationship.

It is not a good idea to use sex as a weapon in a relationship. You should agree to the extent of your involvement. Inducing or coaxing your partner to enter a sexual relationship can lead to negative consequences. Respect your partner's wishes and feelings. It is important that the relationship lasts long and ends on a positive note. You should avoid any form of sexual forcing. This topic has not only personal limitations, but also legal implications.

Honesty is another important aspect of a relationship with a partner in sex. It's important not only for your emotions but also for your health. Talk about this with your partner. Ambiguity is a ticking time bomb and will soon explode. Both partners should be clear about their boundaries and what they expect from each other in terms of physical intimacy. Abandoning this will lead to a bad relationship.

Although sex may not seem like the most important thing in the world, it is certainly one of the most important aspects in an adult relationship. It shouldn't be forgotten. All aspects such as intercourse frequency, medical issues, or other concerns should be discussed in detail.

Deriving Inferences

Deriving inferences is one reason relationships can turn sour. Inferences are when one person does something and the other person interprets it. We are more likely to guess the reason for our partner's actions than ask the question directly. While one partner expects the other to understand, or to express their understanding of certain things, the other partner will expect it. These are all factors that lead to friction. They can lead to a tugowar. Fights which are completely unnecessary or avoidable. These fights could have been prevented by simply asking for the same or stating it. They began because you or your spouse completely skipped the initial step of the ladder. The blame game ensues and the fight becomes inconclusive. These scenarios do not only apply to dating. These situations are common in all relationships, but dating relationships tend to be more sensitive. These situations should be avoided. You need to set limits on assumptions and interpretations. It is important to have a pre-determined truce point. When the fight escalates to a point of no returns, you must have a means to end it.

Sometimes partners begin to take the answers of the other partner as given. Sometimes you feel pressured to say yes, even when you really want to say no. This can lead to difficult situations. It is up to you to figure out how to escape from this trap. These actions can make your relationships unhealthy and impossible to maintain. You should have a plan in place for when you say no. You should never give vague answers. This causes confusion which leads to a relationship that feels burdensome.

Affirmative responses are the best. Silent treatments are more dangerous than fighting and should be avoided. One partner may not understand why the punishment was given, while the other has already convicted the victim and sentenced him/her. Your dating partner must be in constant communication. Establish communication channels to break this lockdown and harness the kisses, make-up and kisses. Whatever your preference, make sure you know how to deal with these situations. They can cause mental turmoil and agony.

Speak up for yourself

It's not unusual for partners to expect support and responses from one another.

There are many times when you might not agree with each other. This is a crucial point. This is a crucial point. Second, support your partner's views and push the partner to follow a route you dislike. Second, be open to your opinion and make sure that it doesn't happen again. The first option is simple but can lead to disappointing and frustrating results, which could cause a rift in the relationship. While the second option might seem harsh, it will save you from future hassles. Healthy boundaries must be established so that your partner does not force you to speak your mind. It may be difficult at first but it will make your relationship much more enjoyable and relieve you from stress and anxiety. Your relationship will flow smoothly and you won't have to deal with the things you don't like. It is the reason they fail. It's easy to avoid it by talking about the things you don't enjoy. This boundary will give you control over your partner. This will give you the freedom to control your personal space.

You won't be forced to like or dislike something. This is easy to achieve in a relationship that is developing into a long-term one. It would be very difficult to stop it later, as it would become a daily routine. It would be difficult to object to at that stage. Unwanted and unintended outcomes would follow.

Cordial Exchange

In all relationships, there would be giving and taking. You must have both rights and responsibilities. An unhealthy relationship can be identified by the fact that there is no exchange. One partner can take full control of the relationship and shift all responsibility to the other. This is where relationships can end. Cordial communication is essential in a relationship. It requires an exchange of ideas, opinions, love and affections. If one person stops contributing, or starts taking too much of the other's energy, then there is less space for them both. It becomes oppressive. To avoid getting to this point, it is essential to define the boundaries of rights & responsibilities. While you may be able to see the pitfalls of these situations, they can also be avoided if there is no clear boundary. The relationship must be governed by you and your partner. The master and the slave should be different. Both of the partners should have the rights to speak up or object when necessary. This prevents one partner leaving abruptly and causing a breakup.

It is possible to have casual relationships, but this is only the beginning of a long-term relationship. It is essential to treat the relationship seriously. You need to set clear boundaries so that you can always have your place, space, and voice. This is crucial. It is important to keep your boundaries firm and remind your partner of them. These are the golden rules for ensuring that your relationship with your partner is on the right path to happiness and remains sweet.

Chapter 3: Classification Boundaries

It is crucial to determine the priority of borders and how they should be classified. It is a great way to create trust and understanding among partners. They provide a lot of space and freedom for couples. You can adjust them to suit your own needs and understanding.

One way to think about boundaries in a relationship is to divide them into three parts.

* Emotional Boundaries

* Physical Boundaries

* Digital Boundaries

A relationship is built upon trust and feelings of love or affection. These are two pillars that make a relationship strong. Both these things are equally important in a relationship. Both are important in a relationship. The majority of cases are where the love lasts, but the trust quickly disappears and the relationship falls apart. People continue to drag their relationships, even when they don't have love. The relationship is not possible without trust. It is crucial that both partners work hard to keep the trust intact. It will always be reciprocal. If you don't want your partner to have access to your smartphone and computer, then you'll need to share the same space with your partner. It would be a sign of trust that your partner is not tempted to take a peek.

The love that a relationship offers must be in abundance. Also, a good relationship must provide love in abundance. It is a partnership of love and companionship. You share your joys and sorrows with your partner. You share your love and longing with your partner. The spark that ignites in a relationship is what matters most. It is vital that the relationship has strong emotional support. However, this support should not take the form overdependence and overindulgence.

In today's fast-paced lifestyle, personal space is an essential need. Respecting the privacy of another person does not automatically mean you are able to invade their space. Respect it at all costs. It should also be respected by your partner. This helps you stay strong and prepared for whatever comes your way. You could avoid breaking up if things don't work out. Respect your partner's personal space.

Your partner should also be able to understand what you are looking for emotionally. You must clearly outline the goals you want for each other. Clear communication is key if both partners want to be honest with one another. It cannot be taken as a general rule. It is important to address trust issues at regular intervals. Your partner should be able to discuss any concerns or fears you have with you. A relationship can move forward with no hiccups if it has this emotional clarity.

Setting emotional boundaries is crucial as it acts as a shock absorber. It's possible to accept small bumps and not feel torture or agony in a relationship. Even in the event of a split, such situations offer a strong emotional cushion. You have better reasons to move on from it without dwelling too much. Both partners must be able to recognize and respect each other's emotional boundaries.

Establish boundaries for codependency levels

The level of codependency that you desire to have with your partner must be determined. You can become a wreck if you are emotionally dependent on your partner. In order to stay strong in the event of a relationship ending, you should have another source of emotional support. Neglecting to have complete emotional control can lead to problems. This boundary must be clearly established.

For the number of sacrifices you are ready to make, set boundaries

It is not easy to have a good relationship without making sacrifices. In order to have a peaceful relationship, both partners need to find common ground. You should set a limit to the amount of sacrifices that are acceptable. This is essential for staying sane in cases where things don't go as planned. Too many sacrifices and then being relegated at the end can make you distrustful about the world. It will also make it more difficult to trust other people in future. To ensure your safety and protect your trust, you should set limits on the number of compromises which you are prepared to make. A long-term commitment is the best option if you're willing to compromise your dreams and goals for your relationship partner.

You must follow your boundaries religiously

It is very easy to blame others while we easily cross our own boundaries. This type of reckless behavior will send negative signals to your partner. Your boundaries should be respected so that your partner doesn't forget their obligation to respect them. The best way to win is to follow the rules.

Physical Boundaries

A common problem in intimate relationships is the tendency to be possessive. If they aren't managed and tended to, these feelings can turn obsessive. This is the most important boundary to keep your mind and body sane. Your partner and you both might want to be free, but you can't resist the temptation of knowing what is happening in each other's life. Although this is not harmful to the relationship, it can lead either to trust deficit or suffocation. It is important that the partners discuss the boundaries they wish to set and the space they are willing to give.

Respect each other's personal space needs

The basic need for personal space exists even when the couple is intimate. This space is necessary for self-introspection, pondering, and reflection. Although you might not be doing anything significant, this space is all yours. It is important to understand that personal space is a requirement for both you and your partner. Respect the boundaries of personal privacy.

Physical needs

Intimacy and sexual relations are part of our daily lives. It is important that both partners reach an agreement. Respect and know your partner's needs. To force or deny someone sexual activity can be cruel. Over time, partners may underestimate this need which can lead to difficulties in relationships. Although you don't necessarily need to be a dictator to have intimate relationships with your partner, respecting their needs and wishes is essential.

Privacy is a must

We all want our secrets to be kept as little as possible. These things aren't secretive or suspicious. They are simply so insignificant for our personal life that it is difficult to discuss. But, when the partner tries to scrub them and scratch them, it can be a problem. This happens often in relationships and can lead to distrust, tiffs and other problems. These things should not be discussed in your home conversations with your partner.

Time

Time is an important commodity. The problem with time is that it tends to diminish as the relationship progresses. The partners may not be willing to wait too long at first. With time, patience wears out. They place less importance on their relationship's time. Everything starts to seem cumbersome from the time spent waiting for the partner to arrive. This is something you need to realize. You have never had the same time. If you lose patience, it can cause problems in relationships. Your relationship with your partner will improve if you take the time to get to know him/ her and show respect for his/her time.

Digital Boundaries

Privacy and personal space are now a very valuable commodity on social networking websites and applications. Today, there is no such thing as a personal information. It's easy to find information, and it's even easier to leak it. The internet makes it easy to clean up the dust of the past. However, some wounds can never heal. Unfortunately, the ghosts and reminiscences of the past will always haunt you and cause problems in relationships. This makes maintaining healthy relationships in your dating life difficult. To keep relationships healthy and functioning, it is essential to set digital boundaries. This will ensure that you don't get haunted from the same ghosts.

Digital Privacy

Some people consider digital privacy essential. It may be difficult to share some facts with your partner. However, you may not feel the same fear sharing it with your friends. Unwanted people can be tagged and viewed on social media accounts that should be off limits. This can lead to problems in relationships. At the beginning of a relationship, you must talk about this with your partner.

You have the option of sharing your social media accounts, passwords, and any other information that you desire or to completely abstain. It's your choice. However, it must be mutually agreed upon. This will stop unnecessary peeking.

You can make it a point to emphasize too many facts about your status. It is your decision to keep it to yourselves, but it has to be mutual.

You must remember, however, that even though you do all of these things, there is always a risk. A relationship does not come with a guarantee. Risk increases when partners split up. It is vital to have some digital boundaries.

Password Privacy

Passwords are confidential and should not be shared. This is not a smart decision. This could lead to a relationship going south. In addition to this, your relationship may not be fully understood by your partner. It is possible for your partner and you to post items from your digital accounts.

Sensitive material should always be handled with care. It is forbidden to share videos or pictures online. Even if your partner consents to them being posted online, it should be avoided. The internet can be a vast and expansive space. You can't lose things on the internet. But you can lose your relationship. This could and will lead to problems in the long-term. You can avoid this bad habit and keep your relationship safe and happy.

This will enable you to have a better relationship and allow you to breathe easy.

You can keep your peace and security intact by setting clear boundaries in your dating relationships. If you are able to set healthy boundaries, it will increase your self-regard. Nobody can treat you as a doormat, or take your self-worth for granted.

Sharing your information is done slowly and securely. This will allow you to take your time, trust your partner, and it won't be too overwhelming. You can decide how much information and how many.

Unwanted interference is preventable and it's impossible to encroach on your personal space. This is something that will pay off in the long term. Your chances of your relationship getting toxic increases if you compromise your personal space.

It is important to establish healthy boundaries so that you can share rights and responsibilities with others in a responsible manner. You can't let bitterness result from a disproportional division. You can limit how much one partner can have for the other. This helps to ensure that a healthy and happy relationship can last for many years. Even minor rifts and misunderstandings could be disastrous for a couple.

You are able to choose whether you want to say "Yes", or "No," as per your preference. You won't be forced to agree with someone else's ideas. It will not be your obligation to follow the words of your partner. This is a great relief, as many relationships lose the voice of one partner, and it fosters resentment. This is not good for healthy relationships. A healthy boundary on authority and intrusion is vital in a romantic relationship.

Chapter 4: Setting Bundaries: Questions Coming Up

You can easily make a long-term relationship work by setting healthy boundaries. Even if your intention is to have a relationship for a while, but you don't want it to last, boundaries will help you keep your mind safe and sound. Boundaries are essential to ensure your stability and ability to handle any circumstance. You don't risk your safety and are not placed in an unsafe situation. If you are clear about your boundaries, your partner will not exploit you beyond the limits of reason. Your emotional anchors are well-anchored and you'll have people and things to refer to in case of an unhappy relationship. Boundaries protect you from being exploited in any way. Boundaries serve to protect you from unwanted physical exploitation.

Each person must determine their boundaries according to his or her needs.

While one may have the right boundaries, it might not work for the other. A dating relationship must have common ground between the partners.

However, we often find that people still face security, mental and emotional problems even when there are boundaries. Inadequate boundaries are the primary reason. You might not give enough thought to it, or overemphasize certain parts according to your convenience. This can be detrimental to your relationship with your partner.

Despite the existence of boundaries, the main reasons why a relationship is not working out are:

Ambiguity

A half-hearted approach to something can lead to it being even more difficult than not doing it. The same applies to boundaries. Consider a scenario where you have a prenuptial deal with your spouse. But the terms listed in the Prenup don't make sense and are contradictory. Who would it benefit? The end result will be more problems and confusion than solutions. The same applies for unclear or weak boundaries.

Ambiguity in setting boundaries for a dating relationship can make it difficult to stick to them. Regular breaches can weaken your commitment and desire to follow the boundaries. Ineffective boundaries, or those that have been set merely for the sake of rules, are unacceptable. It will lead to marital discord. It is crucial that you set clear boundaries and ensure your partner follows them. Frequent breaches of boundaries should not happen and it should be discouraged. These boundaries should be explained to your partner and made clear by you.

Malicious Intent

They must be set with the right intention. These boundaries will work well if they are set to promote a healthy and satisfying relationship. However, if the intention behind the boundaries is control over your partner or to place unnecessary restrictions on them then they will be a failure. Your partner will begin to feel the suffocation sooner rather than later if such intent is not kept secret. You must avoid this practice at all costs.

Some people are natural control freaks. This is difficult to give up and extremely taxing for the partner. This behavior should not be allowed to continue under the pretense that there are healthy boundaries. You should always establish boundaries in order to allow space for each other, foster trust, and keep the relationship alive.

Poor Communication

Healthy communication is an essential ingredient of a successful relationship. Even if your communication is not good with yourself and you do not give your self enough time for reflection, it can lead to bad decisions. You will be frustrated and discontented. This happens if it's with another person with different thoughts, needs and minds. Effective communication is key to any relationship. Without communicating one's needs and advantages, boundaries will not work in a positive way.

Partner must also be aware of the need to set boundaries. Talk about the breaches often. To ensure that boundaries are properly managed, healthy communication is essential. This helps to prevent misunderstandings and disputes.

Inconsiderate Behavior/ Negligence

Be the change in the world. This is the most important way to communicate the importance and necessity of following boundaries. To get your partner to respect the boundaries, you have to do it yourself. Discord will result from careless or inconsiderate behavior. Your partner will be more likely to disregard the rules if you are negligent. It would be unpleasant.

Boundaries are there for your protection. They protect you from any harm. They protect you from harm, physical or mental. However, you are exposed to risk if they are not followed. It is important to avoid such behaviors.

Frequent Breach

If you break boundaries often, it is an indication that your partner doesn't respect or care about them. This will discourage your partner from adhering to them. For not being efficient, boundaries should not be blamed. This is your fault, not your partner. Rules cannot be broken on their own. Broken rules can make them ineffective. In a relationship, it is crucial to avoid breaking the rules or being manipulated.

This will assist you in maintaining a better relationship.

Summarising...

A dating relationship can be very fragile. It is very delicate because it does not have obligations or liabilities. If there are no boundaries, it is more likely to over-commit or not pay enough attention. Both can lead to discord in a relationship.

You can maintain healthy relationships with your partner by setting healthy boundaries. A relationship that is filled with understanding, trust and love. It will be more meaningful, lasting, and memorable. If that is what you desire, these tips can help.

PART II

BOUNDARIES in MARRIAGE

Marriage is a sacred union between souls. But, it does not necessarily mean the complete unification between mind, body, emotions. A social contract is formed when two people marry. They vow to support each other. They agree to share the joys, sorrows as well as pain and sufferings of one another and work together towards improving each other's lives. This is a very holy relationship. Such sharing requires understanding, care, love and trust. This must be maintained for a life time by both spouses. It is important to establish healthy boundaries within a marriage that foster trust, love, and understanding.

For a marriage to be successful, it is important to maintain healthy boundaries. A marriage is functional only if the two partners are respectful of each other's boundaries. Envy, jealousy or competition can all be controlled. Both parties have their own space and feel free to be themselves.

Marriage is a long-term commitment. It is important to play by the rules when you are looking for long-term companionship. This helps to keep you focused and keeps your mind clear.

Boundaries allow you to build trust and respect in your relationship. Boundaries can also be used to help you better understand your partner's needs and feelings. As there are rules for this, you should not neglect the important things. You have a lower chance of your spouse being hurt physically, mentally or emotionally. You have the opportunity to rekindle your love from time to again, and it will not affect the spark or love you share.

People who have the misconception that married couples should not share boundaries are grossly misinformed. Two people can never be complete amalgamated by the simple virtue of a Social Contract. Only when both the individuals and their relationships are in sync can it happen. Harmonious relationships can reach that stage but you have to adhere to certain rules in order to maintain it. These rules establish healthy boundaries in marriage.

Boundaries in marriage are a source of security and contentment. They are not there to limit, but to be liberating. They take away your worries. For instance, boundaries that require you to maintain fidelity bring peace and stability in your marriage. Trust and peace of mind can be achieved by establishing boundaries that prevent you from seeing each other's phones. A marriage that has sexual boundaries helps build trust and admiration.

Each boundary you create must have a purpose. It is important to be honest and clear when setting boundaries. It shouldn't be established to control anyone, but to provide more freedom and breathing spaces.

Modern life goes beyond the four walls and boundaries of the house. To be able to make a living, both spouses must leave the comfort of their homes. They each have their own social circles and responsibilities. Boundaries allow for a healthy work/life balance. Nobody would want to carry the load of pushing the cart.

The following chapters will address the importance of boundaries in marriage, and the consequences they can have.

Chapter 5: Parameters - Setting Healthy Boundaries In Marriage

While you build boundaries, it is essential to understand that they are only for you. If you begin to set boundaries for your spouse, it can become difficult and controlling. This will make your partner feel suffocating. You must set boundaries so you don't cause unwelcome intrusions in the personal space and privacy of your spouse.

Unacceptance and lack of respect for one another's privacy is the most common cause for marital problems. Couples think they can control their partner's life. This can lead to conflicts, rebellions and deception, as well as lies. One spouse forgets some things are better left unexplored, and the other becomes conscious and defensive. This is a recipe for conflict, discord, and distrust.

Boundaries are not intended to be used as a barrier between people. They can also be used as a way to keep you in. Boundaries must be reciprocal when established in a partnership. It is important that you also expect the same things from your spouse. Your boundaries should be healthy and clear.

They should never be used to limit the freedom of the spouse. They should not be used to rule the relationship. It should be a direct principle that you and your spouse can interact in a respectful manner. It should govern your actions and behaviour. You would begin to see the same change in your spouse.

Your boundaries should not be used to force your spouse. They should inspire. It should foster mutual admiration and sweetness in the marriage. It should be possible to set boundaries and prevent intrusions. However, it is also important to agree on the definition of excesses.

It's not easy to set boundaries. These boundaries are meant to make your partner aware about the things that you don't enjoy. These boundaries are what you will not allow your partner to expose to. They can also be used to guide your partner's behavior. Setting rigid boundaries can be hard. It can be difficult for your partner to discuss things with you if you are too clear-eyed and explicit about these boundaries. Their partner might seek out people outside the marriage to help them, and this could be a problem. A good balance of what to take in and what to keep out is essential.

In general, marriages operate on the principles cause and effect. One thing leads another, and then to another. Instead of taking responsibility, we blame our spouses for our actions, attitudes, thoughts, and feelings. This leads to conflicts. Clear boundaries show where your responsibilities end, and yours begin.

It is important to realize that you don't have total control over how others behave towards you. However, you have complete control over how you respond to people.

Remember cause and effect theory. You can create ripple effects by rebutting angry people. Words and actions can have a ripple effect so it is important that you pay attention to them.

Realistic boundaries should be established in marriage. Unrealistic boundaries can lead to frequent trespasses. Your objections can make your partner defensive or overactive. Your boundaries should change and make you a better individual depending on the circumstances. This will bring about the necessary change in your partner. It won't work the other way.

Your boundaries should allow you to:

* A voice to tell you "Yes" and "No" when it feels right

* Power and control to make sound decisions without interference or objection

* Your spouse must be able to understand that they are an individual with a voice

* You can take responsibility for what you do

* You have the power to block unwanted intrusions into your private space

Healthy boundaries mean being able to accept and share differences with respect. These boundaries strengthen marriages and make them more satisfying. But you should remember that such boundaries can take time and patience. It will require a lot effort. Each boundary must be worked on carefully.

The following chapters will outline the types of boundaries you should establish for a successful marriage.

Chapter 6: Personal Boundaries
IN MARRIAGE

Respect for the individual boundaries of each partner is essential for a couple. The couple must respect each other's boundaries. The couple can spend more time together and get to know each others better. They know each other well and are able to identify their strengths, weaknesses and likes. This makes them vulnerable to hurting each other. Even a slight overindulgence can make one partner feel uncomfortable, humiliated, and vulnerable. It is crucial that each partner respects the boundaries of the other partner.

Don't expect your spouse to change their behavior

Human nature is prone to customization. We desire things to be exactly how we like them. We can make this choice with material things but not with our partners. It's futile to force a partner into changing some bad habits. The partner may become defensive or bitter if they are forced to change. Try to adapt to your partner's needs or not expect your partner change overnight.

Don't throw unnecessary challenges

Ignorance is bliss. It is possible to ignore excesses committed by others. However, this may make it difficult for us to accept the behavior of our spouse. These actions look intentional, and that is the reason why they are so common. This will only lead to bitterness. Because you know that your partner did it on purpose, they will likely take offense. Although it may appear as a challenge, the action could be taken seriously. These challenges should not be thrown at you often. It is important not to test such boundaries.

Respect your time and avoid embarrassing situations

Even though the husband and his wife share everything together, there are still moments they might want for their own. If you suddenly appear to be walking in on your partner while he or she is doing something, it could make them feel embarrassed. The other partner might be embarrassed if you go to the toilet when your partner isn't using it. Another example is asking your partner to do something, even if they refuse to do it. Be careful not to embarrass the partner.

Dependence: Is it too much? One thing to think about.

Interdependence is the key to marriage. It is possible for two people to live hand-in-hand together. It is possible to become too dependent on one partner and feel like an undue load. Even if a partner can do it, that doesn't mean they can do it every single time. Overdependence can create frustration and pressure in your relationship. It's not healthy for your relationship. It is important to keep this in mind as you make requests for your partner.

Never cross the boundaries of mutual respect

Respect and trust are key ingredients in a relationship's survival. If each partner is respectful of the other and feels respected, even if they do indulge in some luxuries, it will be a relationship that lasts. The relationship provides security and warmth. If respect is removed from a partnership, the glue that binds the two quickly dissolves. This can have a devastating effect on any relationship. Respect from the outside world is something that both partners should always remember. Mutual respect must never cease. Every effort should be made to keep the relationship intact or to increase it. This ensures that the relationship is healthy.

Marriages that have healthy boundaries between the spouses are happy. Respect, harmony. Trust. Love.

Chapter 7: Emotional Boundaries
IN MARRIAGE

We value emotions. They are part of what makes us human. Emotions are very important. However, it is equally important to know their limits. Emotions are easy to hurt. The problem is that people can feel hurt differently and it all depends on what situation they are in.

A couple that is married is often very emotionally attached. The more time a couple spends together, the stronger their emotional bond and dependency. An attachment will be stronger if there is involvement with children, assets, liabilities, years of shared time, and social bond. However, the more strong the bond, the more susceptible we are to being hurt. That is simply because you have very high expectations. Your partner is likely to expect certain actions and things from you. They can also get hurt if you do not meet their expectations.

Limit Your Expectations

Your expectations should be set in a way that is realistic and helps you keep your marriage strong. The higher your expectations, the greater the chance of disappointment. This isn't good for any relationship, but it is especially bad for marriage. Married couples have no other options.

Separate Your Feelings & the Feelings of Your Spouse

This is not an easy one. This may seem daunting, especially if you live together and share all your resources. The danger of having problems is increased if you allow your emotions to be influenced by your partner's moods or emotions. This can also lead to a loss of individuality. You might not be able support your partner when they need it, as you are likely to be in the exact same position. Before reacting, analyze the situation objectively and attempt to defuse tensions. This is a boundary that you should set.

Be aware of the choices you make

You are not expected to submit to the demands of your spouse. It is part and parcel to married life. It is possible to lose your rightful voice and end up frustrated or humiliated. You must be able to use your voice and choose whether you want to say "Yes", or "No", as you please. You should not force your spouse to say what you think or say.

Control and Manipulation

Boundaries provide you with some rights, but it is important to exercise caution when using them. If people use boundaries as an excuse for manipulating or controlling their partners, the chances of problems increasing exponentially.

For peace in the marriage, use emotional boundaries. Your boundaries should serve two purposes: to protect your thoughts and to preserve your emotional sanctity. Your boundaries should not attempt to control or influence the thoughts of your partner.

Chapter 8: Sexual Boundaries Marriage

Sex is very important

Carnal urges can override all else. They are so powerful that they can wipe out entire empires. The same thing can happen to your marriage if your sexual needs are suppressed. However, not acknowledging your partner's needs and expectations can have the same effect.

The gift of sex is the gift of the man. It is not used for procreation. A relationship can be strengthened by the passion and enjoyment that this act brings. Your marriage will be stronger if you use it. In a marriage, sex should be given a high place. Sex is everywhere in the age of the internet. Sex is being served everywhere in any form, even though the opposites are objectified. This keeps us sexually charged. The problem is that if the partners cannot have a natural and complete venting of their sexual energy within their marriage, they might turn to outsiders. You can solve this problem by giving equal importance to sex within the marriage. Consider it an important catalyst to help you see things in a positive light and things will begin to fall into place.

But if you begin to attach too much value to sex, and stop crossing sexual boundaries, problems can occur. This can cause a crisis in your marriage. Sex is only a means of attaining pleasure and happiness. It isn't the end and will never become. It is essential to understand the boundaries.

Sex is one the most debated but least talked about topics. There are many reasons. The restrictions imposed by religions are explained in a different context. These rules are often misunderstood and incorrectly interpreted. Sex has been taboo since the beginning. When discussing a sexual fantasy, there is always the risk of ridicule and embarrassment.

These things force even married partners not to voice their opinions and to continue compromising. This does not mean life will be happy or content. They look outside of the marriage for fulfillment. It is possible to find it outside of marriage if you have at least discussed it.

Successful marriages should have open discussions about sex. This helps to determine boundaries and understand the needs of each partner. You don't have to look for another partner to create a happy and fulfilling relationship. However, you should be able to focus on your needs and desires while you are there. Remember, this is an activity for both the partners. Therefore, the final product should also be acceptable to both.

Know your partner's sexual needs

A marriage can become frustrating if you don't get it right or in the way that you want. Not understanding your partner's limitations and needs will be a huge mistake. This will result in dissatisfaction or discontent. Discuss this topic with your partner.

Be open to sharing your sexual needs, preferences, or fantasies

Learn to understand your partner's sexual preferences and fantasies.

This will enhance your relationship and help you bond more deeply. Sexual satisfaction is essential. It can make you calm and joyful. You will have a smooth marriage if your partner accepts your sexual desires and you respect your partner's boundaries.

Discuss Anything Without Fear

Partner may harbour sexual fantasies and desires but may not want to openly discuss them. The greatest fear is that you will be ridiculed or rejected. Talking about it with your partner is the best way to learn. Listen to your partner, and be open to their opinions. Perhaps your partner agrees with you. You won't be able to tell without talking.

It is crucial that spouses in a marriage talk about such fantasies openly. It is important to have open and honest discussions with your spouse in order to find a balance. It is important to not be a burden on your partner, or to force their desires. Your boundary should be reaching out and understanding.

Tiger and Tigress at You

Pornography gives new meaning to sexual desire. It has increased the expectations levels to the point where most people feel a sexual frustration. It's impossible to attain, but it can be enjoyed. A small proportion of people will spend more than 10 minutes in bed. Not only that, but all women can indulge in multiple orgasms after having an intercourse. Pornographic content online is full of all kinds of sexual pleasures, such as fab bodies or endless sexual prowess. It's a mistake to think it is real and expect the same in your bedroom. It will result in discontentment and frustration.

Your energy must be channeled in a way that allows you to enjoy the time you have with your partner. The sex should make you feel relaxed and good. The roles, time and examples given by actors are not real. It's not possible to duplicate it. It is never fun, even for actors who have spent hours shooting a 15-20 minute sequence. This is all fake in order to get more sexual desire and make some money. Expect the opposite from your partner.

Your expectations should be set limits. Discuss your sexual desires with your spouse. Let your spouse know what you desire from sex. Explore new things with your spouse but do not force them to try them.

Raising ridicules about your spouse's sexual performance, energy, vitality, and other issues is a grave error. This will result in your partner feeling less sexually attractive and libido. It will make your partner feel ashamed, which could lead to tensions or rifts in the relationship. This is a sensitive subject that can directly harm the EGO. This is a very delicate issue and you must be careful.

Know the Sexual Requirements

Some people have a great appetite for sex. Others find it less pleasurable. Understanding your partner's requirements is the key to marriage. Your demands should be regulated. Look for common ground in satisfaction.

Time of Action

Some people feel the strongest desire for sex after hours, while others enjoy sex in the morning. It all depends on who you are. It is crucial to acknowledge your partner's needs and not your own. It is important to realize that sex has a physical component. It is important. The impulses are not voluntary. The perfect timing will allow you to get maximum pleasure, satisfaction, warmth, and happiness. The problem is that both partners might have different body clocks. It is essential to reach an agreement on the timing of the meeting if that is the case. It is important to agree so that both parties can get the most from their time. You can share the timing, or you can find other ways to make the most of the irregular timings. You can keep the spark going by understanding the limits of your desire and not trying to force them on your partner.

The Extent

This is yet another contention. It varies from person-to-person. Some people may be able to experience sexual excitement 24/7, while others might need frequent breaks. You don't want to make your partner feel guilty about forcing them into sex. It will not make you happy or be enjoyable. Both partners need to be able to understand and agree upon this limitation. The relationship will be bitter if it crosses this line. Marriage is about harmony. It isn't about competing but singing together. You can complement each other's weaknesses. You can assist your partner with these shortcomings. Don't push your partner; encourage him/her. Don't pressure your partner, but encourage him/her to have confidence.

Variations

The fascination with pornography has increased people's willingness to experiment. It's absolutely okay. It's okay to experiment as long as they agree to it. Be aware that your spouse's willingness to experiment shouldn't become a liability. Remember that the final result of an activity is always the identical. The journey to get there must be pleasurable and agreeable to both of you. You can indulge in all your sexual fantasies, including BDSM, kinky fetishes and role play. Be mindful of your spouse's boundaries. This will make it worth your time.

Because of the blinding effects of pleasure, it's easy to cross sexual boundaries. Such breaches must not be taken lightly. It is essential to find common ground. Preventing egos becoming hurtful is the most important thing. You should never say or do anything that might hurt your partner's feelings. This can lead to unusual tensions. It could not only alienate your partner but also make sex less enjoyable. Also, there are more chances for violence and mistrust. When love begins to deteriorate, trust deficits can occur. This is why you must make every effort to ensure that your marriage does not suffer from such problems.

Consider sex as the most important aspect of your marriage. It will make your insecurities disappear. It will create a strong bond of trust and love. Mutual respect will also be increased. The sex keeps the spark alive in a marriage. It is a great way to stay motivated and stimulated. It can revitalize your mind and body. A lesser aspect of marriage is not a good idea. The most important thing is to learn and respect the boundaries of sexuality while striving for the best in your marriage. You could face serious consequences if you breach these boundaries.

Chapter 9: Boundaries In Marriage To Bring A Work/Life Bridge

Human needs and desires are at their highest point now. We all want the very best for ourselves, our families and loved ones. This makes earning a lot of money a must. Your work hours can be long and the workplace tensions will never leave your mind. However, this can adversely impact your marriage. It can be hard to strike a balance between home work and your professional life.

This job was quite easy in the good ol' days. In the agrarian economy, the husband worked alongside his wife in the fields. There was no boss outside the home and only limited interactions with the rest of the world. This created love, security, as well as trust. There were no extreme work pressures, and there weren't strict deadlines. However, the amount of material wealth that was possible to be achieved was limited. There was more contentment in life. The times have changed.

Society works like a pressure cooker. Your direct competitors are your peers in this. It is either power, wealth, position, or power. This is the maddening race to achieve and surpass. There's a rat racing going on, and you're a part. You put in a lot of effort to win this rat-race. You persevere and get your mark. Finally, you are ready to take your vows. You will not be the same person from now on.

Your career was your only commitment. You only had one obligation: your work. And you were getting direct benefits and appreciation. This is very satisfactory. You could quickly forget the anxieties and tensions in the office and go about your day. Nothing is personal or sensitive. You have the right to change your office or company at any time. In a marriage, however, things may be different.

Marriage is a long-term commitment. It is not always easy to be married. There is no direct return on your investment. You might get criticized sometimes, even if you do everything right. Your hard work at the office may be disregarded at home at times. Your commitment to work may be seen as a hinderance to your family. Sometimes, your relationship with colleagues and friends might become misunderstood.

There will always be a tightrope to walk. This applies to all couples in the world. The rules of engagement remain the same. The only things that make a difference in a relationship are trust, understanding, empathy, and love. These must come from both partners. You will need to prioritize. You'll need to know that your presence in a place, especially at home, should be continuous. Even small amounts can make all the difference. To achieve a balance between work and life, it is necessary to create clear boundaries.

It is important to start by setting parameters and rules

Professionals can be so obsessed with their work that it is difficult to let go of their thoughts. This can cause marital problems. Couples may lose touch with their partner if they feel the lack of connection. To keep your work up until office hours, make a rule. Although this takes practice and a lot of hardwork, it's possible for professionals to do. You will be able to spend quality time with your partner.

Pay Attention To Your Partner

Extroverts and people who are overachieving can have the problem of wanting to multitask. This approach can make it hard to maintain a loving marriage. Your spouse will soon feel ignored and bored. At home, be attentive to every little thing that is happening in the household. Support your spouse during the work. Listen to your spouse and open up your heart to him/her. This will create a stronger bond and enable your partner to better understand you. This is a way for partners to be able to sympathize and understand the other's position. If you ever feel stuck at work or down, you will always have someone to turn to when you need it.

Learn to be flexible and understand your partner

Sometimes corporate life is too hectic to allow for breathing. It can be exhausting for you and your partner to have to attend meetings, make presentations, travel, or manage schedules. There will be occasions when you cannot attend an important event. Instead of getting into a fight, learn to be patient. You can forgive your partner for little mistakes and learn from them. By being open-minded and understanding, you can avoid a defensive mindset in your partner.

Make Time for Your Spouse to Go Out

You'll have to make time for yourself every now, then to revive your relationship and the spirit. This will allow you relax and help strengthen your relationship. Find this time and share it with your partner. This will allow for you to relax, regain your energy and give you the chance to recharge. It will also allow you to review the bad decisions you've made.

Marriage is not a one-size fits all relationship. Making mistakes is part of the journey. Learn from them to strengthen your bond. The holy union created in heaven becomes a reality in this world. However, materialistic pursuits may hinder the strengthening of this bond. It is important to draw boundaries between your professional life and your personal life.

Chapter 10: Digital Boundaries In Marriage

This is the age that social networking and constant exposure has become. Everyone wants the title of "popularity". You no longer need to possess certain traits to be popular and famous. With just a few photos and videos you can become a viral internet star or social media superstar. While this has been possible for many, it can also be costly.

It can be dangerous to post intimate pictures, reveal too much information, or increase your marriage's trust. There are certain things that must remain private between the husbands and wives. Your spouse won't appreciate it, nor does the world. However, those who do so face serious consequences.

The internet and social networks in particular have consumed a large amount of our daily lives. The impact of social networking on our lives has been incredible. This could mean that you have to sacrifice time with your spouse to be able to use the internet. This could lead to your spouse feeling frustrated and anxious. It could also lead to a strained relationship.

It is essential to have healthy digital boundaries. It would not be possible to negate the importance of digital media. The internet has made many things possible in life. You should be able to access social media to keep in touch your family and friends. You may also feel jealous, nosy or contentious from the content on social media. The same feelings could be felt by your spouse. It can be very dissatisfying to spend too much time on social networks. Your life can be ruined by the unrealistic, but positive, images of others via social media. This would be a terrible thing for any happy marriage.

These are three crucial digital boundaries that must be observed in marriage

Unhealthy is excess of any substance

While social media may have some advantages, this is still a clear indication that it can be addictive. Social media addictions can be just as destructive to your relationship, marriage, or life. It takes away your personal time. It takes you to an unreal world of false representation. You are more likely to feel overwhelmed by peer pressure and do unnecessary things. It is possible to defer important tasks in order to do this.

Limit your access on social media and other digital media. Establish rules within your home to prevent access to social networking sites from certain times. Your partner should not be able to access your social networks while you are asleep. This can make your partner jealous and anxious. This is the number one reason that couples get into an argument. People want full access to social media and their partners should be able to give them all their attention. This holds true for both sexes. This is why it is important to have rules for how much time you spend on social media. To ensure a happy marriage and peace of head, establish digital boundaries.

Respect each other's privacy via social media

Every person's privacy needs are different. Some people want to be open and transparent while others prefer to remain private. However, very few things can be described as "well kept secrets". But, accessing your spouse's social media accounts or peering into their smartphones or computers without permission is probably not a smart move. It is not about finding incriminating proof or not. It is about trust. It takes very little time to break trust if it begins to weaken. The act of looking into your partner's social media accounts is unethical, immoral, and dangerous. Wait for permission from your partner or invite them to look at it. You should not share your partner's social media accounts. It can be very dangerous. Passwords, access to social media accounts, and passwords should always be private. At all cost, it is best not to share them. The tides of time can change any day, and it is easy to make mistakes when things aren't going your way.

Protect your digital privacy. Social media is not a place to share sensitive information. It is important to keep your passwords private and to change them regularly. Avoid including your spouse in your social media accounts.

The greatest problem with social media is the possibility of misinterpretation. There are many misunderstandings. Keep your marriage clean by adhering to the digital security guidelines and social media boundaries.

Do Not Overstep Your Boundaries

Social media is full of illusions. It is easy to lie online or be totally deceitful. You can often find indecent and sexual behavior on social media. This is a crucial boundary to maintain a happy and successful marriage. This could be the first step toward infidelity. It is possible for what may seem to be a harmless and innocent breach to quickly become a very serious problem. This attitude should not be tolerated. Although you can make friends via social media, all of them must be kept within the bounds of friendship. You can endanger your marriage if you give it an emotional attachment with too much importance.

You can't just physically get out of your relationship with your online friend, but excessive emotional attachment can also cause harm to your marriage. It causes discontent and a lack of harmony in the marriage. It weakens your determination to make your marriage work.

These friendships must be ended quickly. Avoid getting involved in any way outside your marriage.

Your online friendships should be limited. It is important to openly discuss such friendships with your spouse. This will prevent you from becoming discouraged. Talk openly. Don't let temptation fool you. It could prove dangerous.

Digital boundaries must be managed with extreme control. The digital world is having a huge impact on our daily lives. On social media, it's easy to misunderstand or misinterpret certain things. Avoiding problems is the best option. One of the best ways for couples to communicate is by establishing digital boundaries.

Chapter 11: Important Points To Keep In Mind When Setting Boundaries

The boundaries do not serve to confine you, but rather to free you. They allow you to be more confident and comfortable in your relationship. Your only requirement is to be firm and truthful about your boundaries. Do not allow your spouse to make exceptions. For a marriage to be successful, it is important that boundaries are honest. Limitations that are set to satisfy selfish motives will not bring about positive results.

These are the most important things to keep in mind when setting functional boundaries.

Set Realistic Boundaries

Unrealistic boundaries could lead to bitterness and disappointment in the relationship. It is important to set realistic boundaries which can be easily achieved by both partners. This is because the goal of these boundaries should be to make your life simple. You need to reevaluate your boundaries if they make your life and the lives of your partner difficult. Your married life will be more enjoyable if you set boundaries that are helpful. Your boundaries should enable you to spend more quality times with your partner, while keeping unwanted intrusions out.

You don't need to set boundaries for controlling your spouse or selfish motives.

Pride and vanity of the human mind can lead to it believing it is superior to other people and has the right to make decisions. It constantly finds new ways to do it and the global colonization race has been part of this expedition. Your married boundaries should not extend this ideology. You shouldn't make your partner feel less humane. They should not be used to control the other. Your boundaries should allow you to help the partners work in sync. There's no need to dictate or control the other. Boundaries are created to allow for two people to have more quality time together and keep any distractions out of their lives. Boundaries are not meant to be used as a way to choose and exclude people or associations from your partner's life. Set boundaries that are fair and honest for both of you. Both partners should have equal input in setting boundaries.

Boundaries shouldn't be an excuse for inaction

Boundaries do not serve as a guideline for living, they are guidelines and not directives. Boundaries shouldn't be used to preach from the mountain. You don't have to do the chores for your partner. Limitations should not be used as an excuse to stay idle. Boundaries should inspire and bring out the best in people and not make them feel bad.

Boundaries shouldn't be used as a shield against cutting-off communication

Marriage has many unwritten rules. Rules of intimacy are another example. The boundaries you set can allow you to control time, frequency, or other factors. This will keep the spark alive, and you can give yourself enough time to make it work every day. These boundaries shouldn't be used as an excuse for a strained relationship with your spouse. They should not be used for sexual starvation. The boundaries should encourage more longing. You cannot save yourself from being intimate.

Never use Boundaries for Punishment

All of us at times give the silent treatment for our partners to help them see their errors. They are useful for helping the partner to see their errors, but half the world doesn't know this. The treatment is still effective and being used across the globe. To use boundaries to punish your partner's mistakes can be cruel. Marriages need to have open communication channels so that both the spouses can express their feelings. You shouldn't misuse boundaries for that purpose.

Boundaries should not become your cocoon

There are times when everyone wants to feel secure and safe, but we don't have to answer or be accountable to anyone. We seek solitude and forgo communication with the rest of the world. These boundaries shouldn't be used as a means to achieve this goal. The purpose of boundaries is to make your partner more open and transparent. Boundaries facilitate honest interaction. Boundaries make difficult questions easier to understand and allow for open communication. Boundaries shouldn't be used to avoid answers and keep others from getting in touch.

Summarising...

Marriage is a long-term commitment. Two distinct individuals come together with their established identities to spend their entire lives together. You can't make the relationship work without taking a vow, and being tied by social contract. It would take genuine effort. The main reason that marriages are so often ruined is because of the inability to adjust. People become so wrapped up in their own thoughts that they can easily cross boundaries. It is often not obvious that they do not realize the consequences of their actions, as they were never responsible for them. Soon, the other partner begins to realize that they have had enough and leaves.

Marriage is a long-term partnership between two people who have learned through mistakes and trials. They will accept and make adjustments for each others. They would be open to accepting smileys from others that they have never tolerated. They wouldn't be doing anybody a favor by doing it. The other partner would do the exact same. It is possible to work together when each partner sets boundaries. Boundaries are a way for them to decide how far they should go. Boundaries keep things together and from breaking apart. They keep the partners together.

Although marriage boundaries can sound restrictive, they are liberating in their nature. They give you the freedom to live your lives as you please and also set some rules that you must follow together. This will help you maintain balance without losing your identity or free spirit.

Any kind of boundary can be set for your marital relationship, as long as your spouse accepts it. It will help you explore your self better and keep your relationship healthy.

You should start planning boundaries in your marriage, if they have not been established. You will enjoy your marriage more and the friction between you and your spouse will diminish.

You will enjoy a happier marriage and be able achieve a balanced life.

PART III

BOUNDARIES - KIDS

Childhood is an important period in a person's life. A child's personality is formed by interactions with their parents and the wider society. How you treat your child will affect their behavior towards society. This makes it more important to establish boundaries with your children.

You must take special care when setting boundaries with your children. You shouldn't be harsh on your child and you should not make it too easy. You should never be viewed as a foe by your child. It is crucial to set the right example for your children.

Your child must learn to assert himself and not tolerate injustice. Self-defense training is very beneficial in this endeavor. The child must see his or her full potential and be able to defend other children. Your child shouldn't misuse their power or bully others. This exercise is essential in teaching your child to recognize the boundaries of power, and what responsibilities they have.

Children soon learn to value independence, freedom, and self-reliance.

They assert their rights but don't accept responsibility for their actions. This is the hardest part for parents. It is important to teach your children that their rights and responsibilities must be balanced. You'll need to explain to your kids that there's no free lunch. They must also demonstrate their responsibility and earn their freedom. The distinction between freedom and rebellion must be made.

Parents around the world are most concerned about their kids' safety. It is a problem that causes sleepless nights. This fear affects every parent. It is one of the most important responsibilities that parents have for their children. From early childhood, when you teach your child how to stand safely and walk the first steps, to teenage driving a car, you're always concerned for your child's safety. This is something you can't trust anyone to complete for your child.

Parents and children can experience communication barriers. These barriers increase as the child grows up and discovers companionship in other people. The gap between the two of them grows as communication becomes more difficult. This is a time when the child's understanding is developing at a fast pace.

Your children will benefit from you setting boundaries. They keep communication open and act as shock absorbers.

Your influence in the daily happenings of the child's lives decreases while your involvement in the larger events rises. It is easier to communicate well with your child when you have established boundaries. By setting boundaries, you can teach your child how not to bully and how not to get bullied. Respect and obedience should remain intact. Your child is on the right road as long as they see you keeping a safe distance from them, but not getting in the way. Healthy boundaries create trust. It helps to build trust and safety in your child.

With your children, you will need to create trust boundaries. Be clear about the boundaries that you want to set up with your children. You shouldn't be too strict, or too gentle with children. The goal is to strike a healthy balance. Most importantly, it is important to maintain emotional boundaries with the children. The children and their parents fall in the various age brackets. With the passage of time, emotions change rapidly in a child. This growth should be managed with care. Forcing your thoughts and will on others can result in uncalled for rebellion.

Raising children is like a rollercoaster ride. While you are responsible for making sure your child grows up to be a complete person, you have no control over what he or she wants. The balance between not being able to control the child's lives and teaching him or her to be safe is what you must do. You can help your child by setting healthy boundaries. You will be in a position to keep your child safe while remaining sane.

Chapter 12: Boundaries Important For Kids

Setting boundaries for children is difficult as a parent. To be able understand what your child will understand and how to follow it, you must get down to the basics. Also, you must explain to the children why they need to listen to what you have to say. The power struggle is something that children in their early stages do not understand. Kids learn how to assert their authority. They need to know the boundaries they should follow and what they can ask. If parents fail to establish boundaries early, their children will not be able to accept any request. They behave in an unruly manner and are not willing to comply with the basic behavior. You'll need to establish the boundaries of respect, decency, and good behavior.

In the beginning, many parents make the error of trying to satisfy all the demands of their kids. They don't understand that all their demands are unnecessary and don't have to be met. They become stubborn with their demands after this failure. They believe they can just win over their parents by crying, whining or shouting. For anyone, the result is not pleasant.

The basic rules of conduct should be taught to children from the beginning. They should be taught that they cannot fulfill all their demands. You can refuse to accept certain demands. However, if a child demands that you not accept, always provide a reason. This will teach children a simple lesson: every demand must have an explanation. Every rejection happens because of a reason. They must work to improve their understanding. By accepting certain demands and accepting conditions from others, you can help your child develop boundaries. This will teach kids to give reasons for their demands, and then justify them.

Encourage them to understand physical boundaries

Safety of children is dependent on their ability to understand and respect physical boundaries. The physical boundaries are something that children learn from an early age. They see the physical boundaries of roads, crossings or dividers. They recognize that physical boundaries are important for safety. They only need your help to understand these concepts. Discuss safety and protection against dangers with them. To help them see dangers, and how to respond to them, you will need to teach them. They will need to learn how to prevent being hurt or attacked on the road. There are many lessons to learn, and the better it is to get started early.

Your child should be taught how to recognize predators. It is important to know the difference between a positive and negative touch. There are ways to recognize that the person you are talking about is not right for your child. It is crucial to educate children about the dangers of sexual predators as well as how to identify them.

It's also important to teach bullying prevention. Bullying occurs in school and elsewhere. It's not a secret. The kids need to be able to recognize it and learn how to cope. They must also learn that bullying is wrong in all forms. Bullying and bullying are not acceptable. They must report it immediately and strongly oppose any bullying.

Create a Framework

Kids go through rapid changes when they're going. There might be difficulties for them in dealing with these situations. Without strong communication channels, and a structure to answer their queries, they might confide in other people. In such a case, they will get the best advice possible.

Maintaining Authority

It is important that you exercise control over your children. A negative example can be set by being too strict or punishing children with punishment. Your children may become afraid and lose trust in you. Be sure to avoid using punishment as a way to teach the children.

It is vital to teach kids healthy boundaries. It can help them to become an ideal citizen.

Chapter 13: Boundaries Of Types

To ensure safety for your children, you must set many boundaries. You need to ensure that your children remain safe and have a supportive environment. This ensures that your child has the opportunity to learn how to handle situations and understand them.

We can seperate the boundaries into 4 major types:

Physical Boundaries to Prevent Harm

These boundaries are important in helping your child recognize danger. They can recognize what could cause harm and learn how to avoid them. The dangers of outdoor play must be made clear to children. Children will be taught to recognize the dangers by you. Traffic on the streets is a problem. Children must learn to play in the yard. Children must learn that safe play is just as important.

They have to be responsible for their safety and that of their younger children. Your children must learn that hitting, punching, and other types of physical abuse is not fun and could cause injury to others. It is important that the children learn to recognize traffic hazards when walking on the street. They should be taught to refuse any type of physical abuse by others and to immediately report it to their parents.

Emotional Boundaries

Children are emotionally attached their parents and to those they love. They must learn to be kind and respectful of others. They must show respect and love to their younger counterparts. Children must learn to love and respect elders. This stage is when you have a strong connection to your kids and must be used to teach them respect for the elders. Your role is to show them how to treat their younger siblings.

Children must learn how to be polite with visitors, and what the consequences are for rude and unprofessional behavior.

Social Boundaries

Teaching children good behaviour is essential. You can motivate your children to be responsible citizens. Children must learn to respect elders and deter mean behavior. Respecting elders, teachers, or visitors to the home is crucial. It is important to explain these things and to set higher standards of behavior for your children.

Communication Framework

If the communication structure between children is not adequate, it can lead to more serious problems. When this happens, children stop sharing their worries and problems. Spend time with your kids every day. Listen to their daily activities and concerns so that you can establish a proper communication channel. It is important to teach children the basics of mannerisms. Beware of yelling, whining, or cribbing. Your kids should feel secure in sharing their thoughts with you. Children should feel comfortable talking to you about their concerns without hesitation or fear.

If you want to teach good values to your children, rewards and punishments go hand in hand. Your children must be praised for their achievements and you should look at their daily development. Each action has consequences. Kids will be motivated to follow through when they are properly rewarded or reprimanded if they do the right thing. This encourages positive personality development.

Chapter 14: Tips To Set Healthy BOUNDARIES for KIDS

Setting boundaries for children can be difficult. When defining boundaries in relationships or marriage, you can also set equal boundaries. But it shouldn't be this way with children. Your primary concern should be to keep your kids safe from harm, but not too harsh. You should not be too gentle, or the children may not know the importance and seriousness these boundaries. You will need to balance again. Be diplomatic while setting boundaries. Kids are more likely to try and defy authority than they are, and this is because they are in an age group where breaking rules can bring them joy. Your child's development is important, so don't let them get entangled in cheap thrills. For teaching discipline, it is important to have clear boundaries between reward and punishment.

Maintaining calm and composure is the most difficult but essential task. Kids can use their excitement as a trigger. Children may become afraid or lose control of their fear. You might fear certain situations but you can't avoid them. You will need to come up with systems to help your kids be more responsible and understand the importance of having boundaries.

These boundaries will be broken many times, so it is important that you remember this. Children will often defy the rules and seek out new ways to challenge your boundaries. Their enthusiasm for adventure is out of their control, but they don't realize the danger they are taking. They don't have that maturity yet so it is your responsibility to be patient. Be gentle with your kids in these situations. Do not use extreme measures. You will soon find that the situation is much easier to control once you have your emotions under control. As your children know how to handle your anger, they'd be less likely to break the rules and become immune. A framework is the best solution to this problem.

You can help your kids create healthy boundaries by:

It is important to plan ahead and think meticulously

Their immaturity and vulnerability are the greatest problems with children. They don't understand the consequences and are not in a position for to make informed decisions. However, the risks are real and can be easily avoided. So you can prepare for what could happen to your kids, it is essential that you plan ahead. It is important to plan for security in advance.

Planning must align with these speculations.

Children are extremely vulnerable and can sense danger when they are not careful. Your job as parent is to make sure your kids don't make mistakes that can put them at risk. These should be your boundaries. But, you shouldn't blindly set boundaries for things that aren't directly related to your children. You should make sure your child is aware of these dangers and what restrictions they must follow. This preventive saves you a lot.

For teaching your children, you can use affirmations

Your approach to explaining boundaries to children is very important. You cannot expect children to be clear about the importance of rules. It is essential to use affirmations when guiding kids about the boundaries. Poor instructions can be ignored or misunderstood. You must always say what you mean. You should not assume that children can deduce the intended meaning. This will make you a serious person. You should use direct language to explain the cause of the actions. This approach will be more understandable by the children and they won't have to excuse themselves from understanding the meaning.

Your Body Language, and Expressions, Can Also Say A Lot

Your body language, facial expressions, and body language are important indicators of your kids' feelings. You don't have to shout when your child crosses a certain boundary. You can communicate your frustrations by using stern body language and looking at the child with harsh eyes. The child will try to avoid repeating that behavior. Children may respond poorly to constant scolding and chiding. They might mistake it for your casual behavior. However, silent treatment works for almost all people. It is possible to display your sadness over the actions, and the child will quickly learn the lesson. If you don't want the situation to get too chaotic, it is a good idea to use firm body language. You can keep calm and collected while being clear on your point. For children, the greatest fear is not the fear that they will be punished but the fear that they might lose touch with their parents. They will quickly adopt the behavior they want when they see that their support system is working.

Don't be negative

There's not much that you can do with respect and motivation in this world. A motivated child is able to perform beyond his limits. However, a scared child may try harder to conceal the mistakes and improve their performance. You can be nasty with your children if they break their boundaries. They will soon start to hide the truth from others and it won't take long for this to become a routine. This would result in completely opposite results to what you want. While your kids may want the same things as you, they are not capable of understanding this. It is easy for them to become second-nature if you are rude and mean every time they make an error.

You can prevent this by remaining firm and explaining to your kids the potential consequences of their actions. You cannot expect your children to arrive at the right conclusion on its own. Don't instill unnecessary fear in your kids. Try to motivate them to correct the mistake if they do it again and again. They may also benefit from a live example that they can relate to and help them understand the consequences. Be aware that your child might not grasp the gravity and consequences of the situation the way you do. It may be hard for them to manage temptations and keep their limits. They'll be motivated to keep the boundaries in place if they are given a clear incentive. Your mistake may be big, but they will always remember you as their parent. They will eventually need someone to trust. If you are too harsh, they may become more aggressive, making it harder for them to control.

It is difficult for everyone at the beginning

Parenting can feel quite frustrated when children keep making the same mistakes or breaking the rules. If the person is breaking the rules or ignoring them repeatedly, it isn't ready for the full understanding or learning. However, before you get angry and start to think about it, realize that your children are not going to behave like adults overnight. It's difficult to control childhood's free-spirited nature. They are only beginning to learn how to set boundaries. There will be excesses and breaks. There is no reason not to be in control of your emotions. Give them some time. Make sure they are aware of the many times they have not adhered to the boundaries. Also, let them know the consequences that failure to adhere to the boundaries can have.

You must instill confidence in your kids' minds that you are there to support and correct them. You must be there to help them learn from their mistakes and guide without becoming overly anxious.

Respecting boundaries, following rules and being consistent are important at the beginning. This is evident in the vast legal correction system. Do not force them to accept all of the rules. Let your children have the opportunity to learn about them and to accept them as part normal behavior. Once this happens, your children will be able to accept the boundaries as a normal part of their lives.

Reduce your expectations and be realistic

It's difficult to train kids for everything. Young children naturally resist. A child can learn things at his/her own pace. Each child has their own learning difficulties and parents should respect that. Your expectations must be lowered in order to not be disappointed. Different age groups learn at their own pace. Learning speed and ability of a preschooler might be different than that of a middle school student. This must be remembered, and siblings shouldn't be compared. This causes bitterness and contempt among children and makes them feel inferior. The age of a child affects how they grow. But you see them all through the same lens, even though they are stuck in the same age bracket. This can be frustrating for the children, but it's not their fault. This is a very important step.

Confirmation is Key

There are certain things that need to be changed into a daily habit. Setting boundaries is one example. Respecting boundaries should be an obligation for kids and not something that is discretionary. This allows the mind to not have to choose between following or not following the rules. It is important to establish healthy boundaries with your kids. You should stop making exceptions. By setting boundaries, you can show your kids that boundaries must be adhered to or there will be consequences. This will help your children to learn that it's not possible. If you continue to make exceptions from the rules that you established, your children may stop taking them seriously. They will think it is possible to change rules as needed and they don't have to follow them. For your children and yourself, you must not make exceptions. It should become a way of life for them as they get older. It will help them to be a law-abiding citizen.

Chapter 15: 7-Step Methodical Process For Setting Healthy Borderies

FOR KIDS

The process of setting boundaries for your kids' future is not something you can rush. If you rush them, they may rebel against you. It is not a good idea to be too soft as this will increase your chances of them rebelling. Overly strict can cause the child to take the punishment as a routine, and may stop responding. You must be patient, steady, and put in a lot effort.

This isn't something you can do overnight. Pep-talks won't help you learn boundaries. You'll need to start from the ground and go through trial-and-error. Each child has their own needs, attitude, and behavior. This can lead to a false sense of security.

These are the 7 golden rules you can use to set healthy boundaries and expectations for your kids. They guide you through the step-by step process of creating healthy boundaries that are safe for your kids.

You can invest quality time in your kids and create a rapport.

It is easier to emulate someone you love. It is difficult to recognize your parental responsibilities one day and establish boundaries. These efforts are futile. Respecting and loving your children is the best way to get them to listen and respect you. Being loved is easy because children have strong emotional dependence upon their parents. But, to earn the respect of your kids, you will need to invest some time. Kids learn most things from their surroundings. Learning from other people will come naturally if you are also part of their environment.

It's important that you spend quality time with children. You don't have to watch TV with them. It will become a part of their everyday life. Being the family provider will not be enough. Your ability to understand and share in the trials and tribulations of your children will increase if you spend more time with them.

Learn about Boundaries

It is not possible to have one solution that works for all children. One solution that was successful with your friend's child might not work for you. This is why it is so important that you really think about the matter. You can gain insights from other parents by discussing the subject with them. You'll be able see clearly what you want for your children and how to change them.

It is essential to have clarity on the purpose of the boundaries as well as the expected results. To ensure your kids are not subject to unnecessary boundaries, you should conduct extensive research.

It is important to know your purpose for setting boundaries. You must also be able to see what results these boundaries have achieved for others.

Both your parenting style and your boundaries must be consistent. It is essential for the success in establishing those boundaries.

It is essential that your children understand the importance of boundaries. This makes them responsible. If your children don't know what the boundaries are for, they won't be able help you to correct the problem. Knowledge can give you a sense of purpose, and you will feel responsible.

Your boundaries should align with your own personal boundaries. Keep in mind that your kids view you as an inspiration.

They will be irritated if you are constantly crossing or flouting boundaries. When you aren't in a position or capable of understanding them, the kids would continue to try to break those boundaries. You cannot set boundaries as a cat-and-mouse game. From the inside, you must have the inspiration to establish boundaries.

Lighten Up

Never place too much emphasis on boundaries. Begin by giving your kids simple boundaries and appreciating their cooperation. Some kids will not be able to comply and you may have to tell them. This will help your child catch up quickly with the boundaries. Your children will be more able to enjoy learning and will not view the boundaries as a burden.

Children may feel frustrated if they have to follow strict guidelines. It may be difficult for children to adjust to this sudden shock.

Start by teaching kids simple boundaries, such as:

Right to Say "No"

This is the main boundary you should maintain. You should have the freedom to say no when it comes to things or people that will negatively impact your kids. No guilt if you say no to negative influences. This will help children to understand the significance of the right. The main reason people are so miserable in this world is because they say "Yes" even if they mean it. This is due obligations, fear of appearance and other constraints. This bad habit can have a devastating effect. This can lead to a negative impact on your child's ability to say no and not to favoritise any negative situations.

Zero tolerance for any abuse

They must teach their children that abuse of any sort should be avoided as it violates basic human rights. To teach them, you can stop or tolerate abuse of any nature. This will help them overcome bullies as well as other negative influences that could propel them onto the wrong path.

Right to Privacy

As an obligation, the right to privacy is an important human right. Your actions must teach children that no one has the right or obligation to invade another person's privacy. It is possible to teach your kids this lesson by asking them to respect the privacy of their parents. This will teach them how to be responsible citizens. Respect your privacy and that of your children is a right you should exercise.

Give room for disagreement

Rebellions develop when there is less room for dissent. Children need to learn from their parents that they have equal rights. They should be able to agree or disagree on matters when they have good reasons. This will allow for open and fair communication. This will show your kids that you can coexist with people who have different views or are not on the same page. Do not try to discredit any disagreement with force. You will find that you have a deeper connection with your children. They will be more open to you. They won't be able to conceal the actions they want to justify or present to them. This will allow you to have a better understanding of their actions.

These are clear and practical boundaries that you can use to help your kids bond and allow for their voices to be heard. Clear boundaries with an open end goal makes things easier for both sides. But it is crucial that you only move towards each boundary one by one. For some, it may be impossible to enforce all boundaries at once.

Set boundaries that are practical and get involved with others.

We are social beings. Our social environment and those around us can influence our character and help to shape our personality. It is important to include others when setting boundaries. Friends of your children, family members, and friends should be aware of the boundaries that you set for your children. They can play an important role in the future by being part of the system and following it. This is not an unspoken act. Your child's development and personality will be shaped by their boundaries. It is a good idea to involve others. You expect the same behavior from your neighbors' children as from yours, so they don't feel left out. Knowing that they won't be forced to conform to unfair restrictions will help you get them to act with sincerity.

Design a way of punishment and reward

Since childhood, everyone has been taught that each action has an equal or opposite reaction. This rule applies to life as well as physics. The kids will be more inclined than others to perform well if they know that they will receive a reward for good behavior in the form of cash or other tangible rewards. When wrong behavior is detected, punishment can act as a deterrent. You can use light punishments like reducing allowances or perks to deter bad behavior. Your children will see that they are not entitled to the same rewards if they break the rules. This is a lesson that will last them their entire life. Children will be taught that actions have consequences. They will be held responsible for their actions. This means they need to avoid doing anything that isn't appreciated.

Don't be afraid to seek out all possible help

Raising children isn't an easy job. With all the modern conveniences and the assurance that you can buy anything, it's hard to trust anyone when it comes down to your kids. They are the one responsibility that you have chosen to take on throughout your entire life. But children grow faster than we could imagine. Sometimes it may be hard to keep up with all the behavioral, mental, or emotional changes occurring in children. Parents should never hesitate to seek out professional help, including from friends and family. Talk to someone if your relationship with children is getting difficult. Psychologists, counselors, as well as parents, can help you to understand the changes in your child's behavior. These professionals can act as your support network and guide you through this time of turmoil. These friends should not feel guilt, hesitation, or fear about offering their help. You can also benefit from the help of the parents of the friend who is your child's best friend, by discussing the changes that are occurring with them. If your child is in trouble or has bad company, you will be able detect it.

It is also helpful to have a constructive discussion with family and friends about these boundaries so that you can identify problem areas and take corrective action.

The activity should help your child to focus on their lives and avoid any danger.

This step-by, step approach can help to address the issue and give you and your children a better shot at success in life and in the world. These boundaries will help your kids become more confident and independent.

Chapter 16: Difficulties Enthusiasm Setting Boundaries W/Kids

Boundaries will help you build the personality of your child. But it's not always easy to establish the right boundaries. Both the children and their parents face difficulties in setting and following the correct boundaries. The kids often violate the boundaries and sometimes it can be very difficult to set them. It would be wrong for anyone to lay blame. Boundaries must be agreed upon by everyone. Boundaries are a collective responsibility. You must provide the right conditions for children to follow. A problem is when they are not able to set boundaries that are solid and consistent.

There are generally 4 causes for children not being able to establish boundaries.

1. Setting Unacceptable Boundaries

2. A lack of clear communication framework

3. Poorly Conceived Boundaries

4. Responsibility is lacking

Setting Unacceptable Boundaries

Sometimes we undermine others' rights when we assume the authority position. We sometimes set unrealistic boundaries that limit or restrict the ability of others to follow our lead. Such boundaries would lead to many breaches. Nature is rebellious in children. They don't like to be held back. Kids' innocent spirit and freedom can make it seem impossible to put boundaries in their path. It is important for parents to realize that the purpose behind the boundaries is to keep children safe and free from harm. You will lose your kids if they start to accept boundaries that are not acceptable. You must set mutually agreeable boundaries if your goal is to prevent boundaries from failing. This will not work without your kids' cooperation. These boundaries should be set with their consent and participation. If your kids are too young or unable to decide for their own purposes, you should explain the importance of the established boundaries. If there is no clear objective, it would be difficult to establish the following boundaries.

To make sure your boundaries work for your kids, it is important to establish acceptable boundaries. It is best to start with a simple goal, then move slowly up the ladder. This will allow your kids to become habitual about following the boundaries and not feel overwhelmed by the restrictions and responsibilities.

Absence of a Clear Communication Framework

The only way to make any system work is through dictatorship. There is no space for dialogue or dissent in such authoritarian systems. Even if the system is working in their favor, people who are under such pressure feel it quickly and start to feel disillusioned. The real problem lies in the lack of alternatives.

If the choices made are good, people will be willing to choose the harder option. Take Popcorn buckets and beverages sold inside multiplexes and entertainment venues. When given the choice, you will likely choose a smaller popcorn bowl or a carbonated soda. A seller who sells more popcorn buckets or beverages will make more profit. You may be convinced by salespeople that the larger buckets are more affordable by using deceitful marketing techniques. This is because even though you didn't want the bigger bucket or had no need for it, you bought it nonetheless. That's because you don't feel pressured or restricted. You were just presented with a lucrative deal for the larger bucket. The smaller bucket was stripped of the reward. The seller can only rely on temptation. It is the same with children.

Do not force them to obey your commands. Offer them the option of riding with any rider they like. It will be easier for them to respect the boundaries because they have chosen it freely.

You don't need to set boundaries. However, you do not have to communicate them. Communication channels must be established so you can express your point of view and your kids can discuss their problems. Communication helps to remove unnecessary barriers when implementing boundaries.

Boundaries conceived in poor ways

All boundaries should serve a practical purpose. They must be precise and well-thought out. If there are too many loopholes in the boundaries, they will fall apart under their own weight. The boundaries should have a clear purpose and be easily understood. It is important to clearly communicate to your children that you don't wish them to play in the streets due to traffic fears. Be clear with your reasoning. If you are unclear, they will take it as an excuse to ignore you. Inform the children that you are concerned about accidents occurring if they go out on the streets. You shouldn't tell the kids that you are concerned for their safety and they should not play outside. The purpose and the meaning of the boundary should be made clear to the children.

The boundaries should be kept in check. You must keep your children on a strict leash. Explain clearly that defiance will have consequences. They can't ignore the boundaries.

Do not put in extra-strenuous or weak boundaries. Both are susceptible to falling apart. Set boundaries that foster the development of your children and protect them. Explain to your children what the boundaries are for. You should explain to them the potential consequences for crossing those boundaries. These steps will help ensure your children stick to the boundaries you have established.

Responsibility is lacking

Children don't mind being negligent and careless. They love to test the limits of patience and seek more space. Some of them might not want to take responsibility for their actions. In those cases, they would likely be more frequent. The idea of kids protesting by crossing boundaries shouldn't be allowed. It is possible to prevent all this by offering other ways for the children to express their discontent. A child who is aggressive or physically abuses another child will not make any difference. You can also take away rights from children who are not fulfilling their responsibilities. This will help them to understand the importance and the perks associated with boundaries.

These are some of most common problems with setting boundaries for children. If you plan carefully and think through your options, you can prevent these problems. Boundaries do not allow for compromises or defiance. Boundaries serve a specific purpose: to enforce certain rules. You should not be allowed to change rules during the game.

While it is vital to convey to children the importance and necessity of boundaries, explaining this to them is just as important for their safety.

The boundaries you set with children must be sensitive to the needs of each individual and should be considered for their uniqueness. They should match the abilities and requirements of the child to ensure their best performance. These boundaries will improve the overall development of your child.

Chapter 17: Understanding Bundaries

What are Boundaries, exactly?

It is crucial to have boundaries in order to live a healthy and balanced life. It can be confusing to understand boundaries and why they are important. But you will get a thorough understanding of the topic. This will include the definitions of boundaries as well as the types of boundary that people should set. A discussion will be held about the benefits of defining boundaries.

What then are boundaries? Boundaries define the boundaries that limit how you behave or interact with others. Boundaries may be physical, psychological, or mental. They protect you against harm. You must set boundaries for your self because others can dictate how you behave which can cause harm to your health.

Boundaries are important as they allow you to control your life. You can decide with whom you want to interact and how. This is important especially in regards to your relationships with friends and family. It can cause you to feel disengaged, resentful, or worse, your relationships with family and friends can suffer.

Boundaries: What are their importance?

Boundaries allow you to take control of your life. You control who you choose to interact and how. This is important especially in your relationships with friends and family. It can lead to feelings of resentment and depression, which can damage your relationships.

Boundaries help you to avoid harm. You must establish boundaries that protect your personal space. You can tell people to stop hugging you if it isn't your preference, and if they still try, you can quickly move away to let them know you don't like them hugging you.

Understanding why you need boundaries and how it can benefit your mental health, well-being, and mental well-being is one thing. It is possible to benefit your loved ones and yourself by setting strong sexual, physical, and emotional boundaries.

1. A strong boundary makes you feel safe and secure. In order to feel safe and protected from others in your life, it is crucial that you set boundaries. If you are uncomfortable with someone touching you or wanting to touch you more than necessary, tell them.

2. You will feel more confident if you set boundaries. This will increase confidence and help you be clear in your relationships as well as at work. A healthy boundary means that others respect you more as

you will have consequences if you don't meet your responsibilities.

3. You can help others respect your decisions by setting boundaries. When they make a decision, they will likely see your opinion as something they should consider.

4. In cases of abuse, setting boundaries can help defuse volatile situations. Always try to work with the other person and resolve the problem without pointing fingers. However, if you are unable to resolve the problem through talking, and the person's behavior becomes more aggressive, you will need to establish clear boundaries. This will prevent it from becoming violent or dangerous for yourself (and others). It is important to stop engaging with people who are aggressive in trying to solve a problem. If someone is like this, it's not worth trying and reason with them.

5. Boundaries allow you to better take care of yourself. This is especially true for mental and emotional boundaries. It is crucial to be mindful of who you invite into your home and with whom your feelings are shared. If you don't set boundaries for your emotions and thoughts, you may feel overwhelmed, drained, even abused when you spend time with certain people.

6. Boundaries allow you to keep your values in check. Setting boundaries protects what is most precious to you and prevents it from being compromised.

7. Boundaries will improve your sex and relationships. If you set boundaries for your partner, it will be easier to achieve these things. Your partner should know what is acceptable and how they can be respected.

8. Boundaries are important for you to become an independent person. They also

help you when someone is ill or dependent upon you financially, emotionally or mentally (for instance, a parent). Consider a situation where someone around you experiences difficult times. You will want to do your best to help them in this situation because you care so deeply. If the person you are helping isn't going to be independent, you should set up strong boundaries that will allow you to live your life as you wish.

9. Boundaries are a way to get rid of toxic people and have healthier relationships. You can let go of someone who treats yourself like dirt.

10. Respecting others' boundaries will help them respect yours.

Types Of Boundaries

There are several types and types of borders.

1. Physical boundaries

2. Emotional boundaries

3. Mental boundaries

4. Social boundaries

5. Sexual boundaries

1. Boundaries of Physical Nature

This means setting boundaries on how close you can be to others. To maintain your personal space, you should set physical boundaries. For example, you could tell people not hug you if it isn't your preference. Or, if they do hug, you can tell them to move on after a few seconds. That will let them know that you don't like being hugged for too long.

2. Emotional Boundaries

It means limiting the influence of others on your feelings and mental state. Setting emotional boundaries is essential because others can influence how you feel by simply being around you. If you have a friend who makes you feel guilty for being with them, tell them you don't agree and you would rather not be around them.

3. Social Boundaries

Protecting your social life means protecting yourself from harm. If you don't wish for people to manipulate your relationships or invade your privacy, you need to set strong social boundaries.

4. Mental Boundaries

This refers to how much others can interfere with you thoughts and opinions. Mental boundaries help you avoid being controlled or manipulated. This can happen if your mental boundaries are not set. For example, if someone tries to change your mind about a topic, you can tell them that you will take your own decisions and won't need their assistance.

5. Sexual Boundaries

This means you will set limits on what other people can touch you. You shouldn't feel guilty for wearing your clothes and telling people you don't want them to touch your body. Your body is yours alone, and no one else can dictate how it should be used.

How to establish boundaries

Now that you are more familiar with boundaries, let's talk about how to set them.

These practical tips will help you to set strong boundaries.

1. Find out the kind of boundaries that you need. As you can see, there are five types main boundaries: physical and emotional, mental, socio-sexual, and mental. The first step is to determine the type of boundary that you need most help with.

2. Talk to people. This is an important step which can be difficult. Talk to those in your life who are affected by your decisions and inform them of your boundaries. While it is likely they won't respect your boundaries at first you need to keep going. This is for your good and will help avoid future conflicts.

3. Be aware of the consequences when you say "No". In the heat of the moment, you often say "Ye"s instead of "No" to avoid feeling bad about not saying "No", especially if the other person you are talking to is close to you. Even though it may seem like there aren't, it is important to consider the consequences before you say "No".

4. You should be empathetic to others who set boundaries. You should be understanding when someone in your circle needs space or tells that they don't wish to talk to you. Keep in mind that you

would like them to understand if the situation was reversed.

5. Your boundaries should be respected. This is the most difficult, but essential step. It can take some time to get used to these new boundaries.

Boundaries aren't only for those with difficult lives or struggling with their mental well-being. Healthy boundaries are good for everyone. They help to create a healthy, respectful relationship between all involved. If you have healthy boundaries you are aware of your limits and also respect those of others. This is an essential part in any healthy relationship.

While it may seem difficult to establish boundaries, it is essential that you do so for your own benefit. You have complete control over your life. You shouldn't feel ashamed to ask for what and set limits. It is something you should be proud of. Do not hesitate to set boundaries and begin living the life that you deserve.

How to enforce boundaries

As you can see there are many good reasons for setting boundaries. They help you to protect your self from harm and allow you the freedom to live your life to your values, which will lead to happier relationships. It is essential that you know how to enforce these boundaries in order for them to work.

Here are some suggestions to help you enforce boundaries and achieve the results that you desire.

1. Be assertive. Be assertive. You must ensure that people respect your boundaries if you are to be effective.

2. Be consistent. Set a boundary and make sure that you keep it. Do not compromise.

To respect their boundaries, people must know what is allowed.

3. Be clear. Clear boundaries will ensure that you are clear about what is acceptable behavior.

4. They can be changed. Boundaries can, and should, change as your needs change and the world around you changes. It is your right to make any changes or modifications to a boundary you have already established. It's your life. You must take charge.

5. They should not be broken by others. If you feel someone is violating your boundaries, let them know immediately. Do not wait to make it unbearable. Otherwise, you may lose the ability of setting limits.

6. Know your limits. You should first consider the reason someone is trying so hard to get past your boundaries. Don't let

someone who uses their temper to get their way be aggressive. This is because they won't listen to you no matter how much you get in your face. You must remain composed and calm in these situations.

There is no universal approach to setting boundaries. The way you do so will vary depending on who you are and what your situation is. The following tips can help you set strong and healthy boundaries for your life.

Chapter 18: On The Lose Without Boundaries

Although it is crucial for your health and well-being many people do not set boundaries. Though you might feel ashamed or scared about setting boundaries for your health, it can lead to much more serious consequences.

Set boundaries can make you feel frustrated, stressed out, and overwhelmed. Your relationships can become dysfunctional and your overall health will suffer. You could also end up in abusive or dangerous situations.

If you feel overwhelmed and stressed constantly, you may lack healthy boundaries.

How do you recognize that you are lacking healthy boundaries?

These are 10 signs that will help you establish boundaries.

1. You feel like everyone is taking care of you and you don't take care of yourself.

2. Even when it isn't convenient for you, your friends, family, or colleagues are always available.

3. You will always say yes to any request, even if your heart is not in it.

4. Do not speak up for yourself.

5. Without judging, you allow people to cross your boundaries.

6. You are always doing what other people want, rather than what you want.

7. You don't feel like you can say "No!" to anyone.

8. You feel overwhelmed and stressed all the time.

9. You feel not good enough.

10. You find yourself in an abusive or harmful situation.

If you find yourself nodding in agreement to any of the signs, it's time to set boundaries. Boundaries can be beneficial for your mental, physical and emotional health. They also help to keep you in good relationships. Boundaries may be inborn or learned.

The Learned and Inborn Boundaries

These two concepts are important in order to create healthy boundaries. While inborn boundaries refer to the boundaries that you are born with; learned boundaries are formed as a response and result of others' attitudes towards, and the society.

Learned Boundaries

How you were raised, the interactions you have with your friends and family, as well as society's expectations about you, can all contribute to learning boundaries. These are boundaries that someone learns from others. The typical example of learned boundary is when a person learns the right or wrong boundaries from others, such as their parents, teachers and other adults. Sometimes, people don't know how to properly set boundaries. This is often due to having had negative experiences as children and being exploited.

Inborn Boundaries

They are the boundaries that you were given. For instance, some people are naturally more introverted than other people and need more solitude to recharge. Others have a natural sense of justice and fairness, and are willing to stand up for what they believe in.

Inborn boundaries are a natural part of children's development so you must nurture them and make them stronger. Unfortunately, many people fail their inborn boundaries.

Toxicity Management

Who is a toxic individual? Anyone whose words or actions bring negativity and distress to your daily life. Toxic people often deal with their trauma and stress. To achieve their goals, toxic people behave in ways that don't show them in the best light. They also upset others. But it can be difficult to recognize toxic people because their behavior can be subtle.

A common way to deal with toxic emotions is to shut out people from your daily life, conversations, and feelings. This is more dangerous than it is helpful for both you and the other person.

Sometimes, you don't want toxicity to be dealt with head-on. So instead of taking the necessary steps to eliminate it or setting healthy boundaries to keep it away, you may entertain them. You may decide to stop talking with someone who is hurting you. You might also stop feeling any emotions (e.g., anger or hurt) around them. This could be harmful since it could make them even more toxic to you in the long-term. It can cause you to suppress other emotions and lead to serious health problems.

In extreme cases, someone's toxic nature towards you can put your life in danger. For your safety and your own mental health, it is best to eliminate them from your life.

Setting Boundaries: A Challenge

It can be hard to set and maintain boundary lines. They require practice and time. They are worthwhile.

Setting boundaries can be difficult. To do it correctly, you will need patience and determination. They're worth it because they can help you build better relationships with other people.

Setting boundaries can be difficult, especially if this is your first time. Sometimes you might feel guilty or selfish. You may be concerned about what could happen if the other person sets boundaries that aren't acceptable or is unwilling to adhere.

However, self-care is about setting boundaries. It is a means of taking care yourself. It is vital for healthy relationships. Setting boundaries shows the other person respect for you and your time. It is also an indication to others that respect and you desire to be treated fairly.

As difficult as it might sound to set boundaries it is necessary. And the good news? It's possible. Additionally, the benefits will last for a long period of time.

Boundary Myth

Because of certain myths, many people struggle to set boundaries. These myths play a role in why people struggle to establish boundaries and keep them.

One of the most popular boundary myths is either the belief that setting boundaries can cause alienation or that it's impossible to maintain healthy relationships while still setting boundaries. This assumption is false.

Respecting other people's boundaries is about being open to sharing your resources and limiting what you are allowed to do. It is about deciding which aspects of yourself are acceptable to share with others. It is also about being open to listening, talking or being available for someone else.

It's important not to forget that boundaries don't have to be placed on others but are guidelines that you establish for your life.

It is not always easy to set boundaries. However, it can bring huge benefits to the individual and the relationships that they are a part of.

Understanding Boundary Myths: How they Limit Your Life

Boundary myths can restrict your freedom and ability to live your life. It is important to realize that there are no right or wrong ways to set boundaries. The important thing is to find the most effective way to establish boundaries. You should also be aware of the possibility that your boundaries will change over time. What worked in the past may not be applicable in today's world. As you get older, your needs will change and it becomes more difficult to determine what works for you. Flexibility and being able to adjust your boundaries as necessary is the key.

Boundary Myths - Examples

There is nothing more liberating that setting boundaries. Setting boundaries allows you to communicate your desires and needs clearly and concisely. Establishing healthy limits is a way to regain your power. Many people have been taught that setting boundaries is unkind or selfish. Many people hesitate to do this because of the negative beliefs they have about setting boundaries.

Here are some common myths that surround setting boundaries.

Myth 1; I cannot set boundaries for people who will hate me.

Reality: Setting boundaries shows respect for yourself and others. Even though people might not agree with everything you do they will respect your choice. People will respect your boundaries if you don't like them.

Myth 2; I won't lose my friends if I don't define boundaries.

Reality: You will make more friends by setting boundaries. These are friends who will honor your decisions and support all of you. They will support you no matter what, and won't take advantage of you kindness.

Myth 3 I'm too young/I am too old to be able to set boundaries for others.

Reality: You can set boundaries at all ages! There is no one age that is right for setting boundaries. As everyone grows up, they learn how to assert themselves. It is just a matter in which age you feel comfortable setting boundaries.

Myth 4: People will perceive me as selfish if my boundaries are set.

Reality: This myth might be one of many reasons why it is so difficult for people to set boundaries. However, self-care doesn't make one selfish. It helps you become more self-aware. Don't allow anyone else to use your kindnesses or compassion for you. This will be detrimental to your well-being. It is true that people care about you and will not allow themselves to be selfish in their kindness. This will not do any good for your self-esteem.

Myth number 5: I'm not mean and don't need boundaries with anyone.

Reality: Everyone needs boundaries, even though you may think that you're too "nice" and "mean" to be there! It is important for everyone to have limits on how much they will tolerate from the people in their lives. This is vital for your mental and physical well-being.

Myth 6

Reality: Conflicts are created when people don't understand what you feel. By being clear about where you stand and what you are willing to accept from those around, conflicts can be avoided. If you don't let others walk all over you then they won't take advantage you. It also means that you will never get angry at them.

Myth 7: I am a compassionate person. I should therefore not have boundaries with those around my.

Reality: One of the greatest qualities one can possess is compassion. But, compassion is not always a good thing. This does NOT make them mean or selfish.

Instead, it makes them fair. You will be happy and healthy if someone cares about you. This means that they will not try to take advantage or change you in anyway.

Boundary myths may be rooted in an underlying fear of saying no or worrying about how others will react if you put a limit or boundary. When someone asks for something, it is easy to feel guilty. But, it is important to remember that boundaries are not a sign that you are uncaring or selfish. The goal of setting boundaries is to find the right balance between caring about others and taking care yourself.

Chapter 19: Be Self-Experienced And Build Linearity

The Journey of Self Discovery

Are you ready to embark on a journey of self discovery? When you realize what you want in life, you can set out to live it. You might have noticed that people who are successful in their career for a lifetime have a common goal. They work hard towards achieving it. They know what their goals are and work towards them. They also know who they are, their strengths, weaknesses, likes and dislikes.

If you don't know what your desires are, it can be difficult to set boundaries. You might be wondering what this means. It may seem strange, but it is essential. What if you don't know your boundaries?

First, you must understand who you really are. What makes you happy What are you most passionate about? Once you've identified your values, it will be easier to create boundaries for yourself. Here are some questions to help identify who you truly are.

What do you want from me?

Why should I want this?

What stands in my way to achieving the things I desire?

What can be done to remove any obstacles?

How can you build your strength over time? Take consistent steps towards your goal.

It will slowly become clear to you who you truly are when you answer these questions honestly. This will allow you to develop a deeper understanding of yourself and what your values are. It is difficult to establish boundaries for yourself without self-awareness. You know yourself well enough to recognize how dedicated you are to achieving your goals. Why would others not respect your boundaries if it seems like they're getting in your way?

If you struggle to answer the questions above, it could be an indicator that you may be selfish at times. This means that setting boundaries and staying true to them, even when you disagree with others, will help you grow as a person.

What is it like to be yourself?

There is no single answer to this question. Everyone is on a different path to self-discovery.

Here are five suggestions to help you find the right place for you.

1. Accept new experiences and meet new people. Experimenting with new things is a great way to learn more about your self.

Go to new places and try different activities. Meet new people. This will allow you to have a more holistic view of your life.

2. Pay attention how you feel and what your thoughts are saying about you. Your thoughts and feelings can tell a lot of things about you and how you view life. Pay attention both to the things you love and those that make your unhappy. What does this say about you?

3. Ask for help. Help is needed sometimes by everyone. Do not be afraid to seek out professional help, whether you are lost or don't know how to get started.

4. Be you. Being someone you are not is a recipe to disaster. It's a waste your precious time, and it will make you lose your true identity. The sooner that you accept yourself as you are, the happier you will feel.

5. You shouldn't compare yourself with other people. Comparing yourself with others is a waste both of time and effort. Everyone is unique, and each person has their own strengths. Don't focus on what someone else is doing.

These are just few tips to help you find yourself. The most important thing is not to shut out new experiences. Listen to your thoughts and feel the pain. Learn from the past.

Self-examination

Self-examination involves the careful assessment and evaluation of one's own behavior and emotions. It is also known by its acronym, introspection. It is a foundational part of all psychological and philosophical theories. Self-examination can help people understand their motivations and behavior and how they react in different situations. It can help identify personal biases. Understanding yourself can be the first step towards changing your behavior for the better.

It can be hard for some people to do self-examination, but it is well worth it. It can help you and others live a more satisfying life.

Self-examination is something you might do for many reasons. It can benefit many areas. It can provide psychological relief from negative emotions such as guilt or anxiety.

Self-examination is a way to find out how much control your behavior has over you. This information can help change your behavior. This can make your life more enjoyable for yourself and others.

There are many options for self-examination. The best one for you is the one you choose. It's important to be honest and open with yourself. This is not an easy job, but it's worth it. You can gain a better understanding of yourself through self-examination. This will lead to a more fulfilling and satisfying life.

The People-pleasing Mindset

People-pleasing tends to be a result of a lack in setting boundaries. People who don't have boundaries feel overwhelmed and stressed because they go around pleasing everyone. Because everybody has different opinions about their life, they are unable to make a choice.

People-pleasers pay more attention to what other people think than they do about themselves. This can lead them to lose sight and forget who they are. People-pleasers can end up being unhappy because they are putting other people's needs above theirs and compromising their happiness in exchange for others. This also stops them from living up their full potential, as they miss out on the opportunities that could help and support them in life.

How to recognize if you have people-pleasing tendencies

There are several signs that could indicate you have a people-pleasing outlook.

1. Even if it is not your desire, you are bound to follow the wishes of others.

2. You can't just say "no", without feeling guilty and feeling disappointed by the other person.

3. People often place others' needs and feelings first, even if that means giving up something they need or want.

4. You may find it hard to be yourself in the presence of others and will change your identity to fit in.

5. You worry about what others think about you and whether or how they view you.

6. Avoid confrontation and conflict wherever possible, even when it makes you unhappy or uncomfortable.

7. You feel that you are unable to be yourself with others and must hide your true feelings.

8. People are constantly trying to please other people, even if this means that you compromise your own beliefs or values.

9. You struggle to make difficult decisions because you want everyone to be satisfied with the result.

10. You are a people-pleaser, because you don't want to be rejected or criticized.

11. It's almost as if you're walking on eggshells all the time around other people.

12. Your opinions and thoughts are more important than what other people think.

13. Sometimes, you may be manipulative in order to get what your heart desires.

How to Change People-pleasing Mindsets

To change people-pleasing thinking, you need to practice self-love. This means that you need to take care of your own needs first, and not put others' needs last. Learn how to say "no", and not feel guilty or anxious. Also, learn how to be more assertive.

Start by identifying and living your core values and beliefs. If you don't have any core values, beliefs or principles, it's time to start looking for them. This can be done through books, classes, counseling, or your own soul-searching. It is important to know your core values and commit to living them every day.

The second step is to establish boundaries with the people you love. This means you have to be clear about what you need and what you want, and then stick to it. They won't respect your boundaries and will waste your time and energy. It's OK to say "no" and not feel guilty.

Finally, you should take care of yourself emotionally and physically. This includes eating healthy foods and exercising, as well as practicing self-care rituals, getting enough rest, and being around supportive people. If you take care for yourself, it will make it easier to take good care of others.

People-pleasing & its Woes

People-pleasing is a common problem that can have severe consequences. People-pleasers, or people who place the needs of others above their own, can lead to serious health problems. You can see this in many different ways. For example, they may be too accommodating or rescuing others. Or they might just say "yes" even though they want to say "no".

People-pleasers are often guilty of feeling a strong sense of guilt when they don't follow other people's orders, even if it would be detrimental or harmful to them. Because they fear saying "no", it can lead to conflict and anger. This guilt can make them feel trapped in unhealthy relationships. In the end, they are subject to criticism and resentment by their loved ones, peers, and romantic partners.

People-pleasers prioritize the needs and well-being of others in order to better understand them and build a deeper relationship with them. People-pleasers can have a great trait, but it can often lead to low self esteem. It can lead to people feeling that they are not worthy of being a good enough person or not enough. This is not true. People-pleasers need not forget that they are valuable individuals, regardless how much time and effort is spent helping others.

How to say no without feeling guilty

It can be hard to say "no", when others' feelings are at stake, but it is necessary. Even though it may be difficult for parents not to say "no", even if their children need them constantly, they should also remember that their children need time and attention. For their own well-being and that of their families, parents must be able to communicate with their children the boundaries they expect.

How to Say Goodbye and Say "Goodbye" to People-pleasers

1. Communication is crucial to making any change in your life. It is essential to communicate with the one you are saying "no", and what your expectations are for their future actions. This will enable them

to make a decision that is clear and understandable.

2. Create a conflict resolution program with the person/people who have been causing conflicts for you. It is possible to tackle the problem head-on. You can also devise a plan for resolving future conflicts that will make both of you feel respected and heard.

3. Be authentic! You can be authentic when you say "no" if it feels right for your soul. In the end, trying to please everyone will lead to a lower mood and feelings of resentment among others for not completing what you didn't want to do.

www.ingramcontent.com/pod-product-compliance
Lightning Source LLC
Chambersburg PA
CBHW050024130526
44590CB00042B/1890